MY LIFE:

GROWING UP NATIVE IN AMERICA

MY LIFE:

GROWING UP NATIVE IN AMERICA

Edited by IllumiNative

With an Introduction by
Crystal Echo Hawk

Entertainment
BOOKS

New York   London   Toronto   Sydney   New Delhi

An Imprint of Simon & Schuster, LLC
1230 Avenue of the Americas
New York, NY 10020

First MTV Books/Atria Books hardcover edition October 2024

Simon & Schuster: Celebrating 100 Years of Publishing in 2024

For information about special discounts for bulk purchases, please contact Simon & Schuster Special Sales at 1-866-506-1949 or business@simonandschuster.com.

The Simon & Schuster Speakers Bureau can bring authors to your live event. For more information or to book an event contact the Simon & Schuster Speakers Bureau at 1-866-248-3049 or visit our website at www.simonspeakers.com.

Interior design by Jill Putorti

Manufactured in the United States of America

1 3 5 7 9 10 8 6 4 2

Library of Congress Cataloging-in-Publication Data is available.

ISBN 978-1-6680-2170-5
ISBN 978-1-6680-2172-9 (ebook)

CONTENTS

CONTENTS

INTRODUCTION

By Crystal Echo Hawk

Nawa (Greetings), relatives.

As with Americans of so many backgrounds, my upbringing was marked by duality.

On the one hand, as a young Native woman, I was surrounded and inspired by the incredible leaders in my family who fought for Native rights and advocated for education, health care, food sovereignty, child welfare, and cultural preservation across Indian Country. They taught me always to be proud of the history and beautiful culture of my Pawnee people. Still, like most Native people, I had to overcome the ignorance of others, facing toxic stereotypes, systemic racism, teasing about my last name, and bullying of all kinds.

Many groups in this country know what it means to be exploited and forgotten. At the same time, we know what it means to find resilience, to heal, and to live with incredible courage, strength, and joy. Over 9.7 million Americans identify as Native. We are innovating and leading in science, fashion, media, politics, and beyond. We are the story of America. And yet, our story is so often untold.

In 2015, I founded and co-led Reclaiming Native Truth, the largest public opinion research project by, for, and about Native peoples. The groundbreaking results exposed our invisibility among the general public and within our institutions, from government and education to health care and pop culture, and beyond. Nearly 78 percent of people in the United States know little or nothing about Native Americans.* This invisibility is what fuels injustices and the harm they create, including the crisis of Missing and Murdered Indigenous Persons (MMIP), "Native" mascots and their impact on the mental health of Native youth, and the legacy of Native American Boarding Schools, through which one hundred thousand Native children were separated from their families and subjected to abuse and forced assimilation.

---

*Reclaiming Native Truth research partner Greenberg Quinlan Rosner Research, in collaboration with Dr. Stephanie Fryberg and her team.

If our invisibility perpetuates harm, the stories of our incredible talent, creativity, and contributions have the power to change the future. Our research became the foundation for a new mission: disrupt the erasure and the stereotypes that continue to oppress us. To accomplish that mission, we needed to create an organization to drive the change, and so I founded IllumiNative with the goal of building power for Native peoples. We set out to foster a world that respects Native sovereignty and self-determination, where Native peoples author and drive our own narrative, and where our children see themselves authentically reflected in the world around them.

Our work is part of a movement of many movements that is shining a light on contemporary Native peoples and sharing with the world our thriving communities. In 2016, the demonstration at Standing Rock shook the world and delivered a message no one could ignore: we are still here. In the years since IllumiNative's founding, we have witnessed and helped drive a transformational increase in the visibility of contemporary Native peoples and the issues impacting our daily lives. More people than ever, and more people in power, are seeing us and hearing our true stories. Together, Native-led organizations, tribal leaders, Native creatives, grassroots organizers, and our non-Native allies are elevating Native peoples nationwide and achieving authentic representation in all sectors of American life.

When Lily Gladstone (Siksikaitsitapii, Nimiipuu) took the screen—and the industry—by storm with her riveting, Golden Globe–winning performance in *Killers of the Flower Moon*, she amplified the experience of the Osage people and also signaled a seismic shift in the Native presence on television and film. Groundbreaking shows like *Reservation Dogs* have earned national acclaim, and Native-driven content like *Rutherford Falls*, *Dark Winds*, *Molly of Denali*, *Prey*, and *Echo* have disrupted our invisibility. They did so by replacing harmful stereotypes with power-building representation and challenged not only how non-Natives see us but also how we see ourselves. For so long, the narrative held that mainstream audiences didn't want to see us on-screen; now both audiences and critics are hungry for Native-driven content.* We have always had the talent; finally, we have the opportunity to tell our stories, and we have so much more to say.

Our progress extends from Hollywood to the highest court in the land, where we are seeing the dawn of a new judicial era in which courts affirm treaty rights and tribal sovereignty. In *McGirt v. Oklahoma*, the Supreme Court ruled that 3 mil-

---

*USC Norman Lear Center Media Impact Project.

lion acres of eastern Oklahoma still belong to the Muscogee (Creek) Nation. In another historic decision, in 2023, the Supreme Court upheld the Indian Child Welfare Act (ICWA), which protects Native kids in child welfare proceedings by keeping them in the care of their extended family or tribes whenever possible, helping maintain their sense of belonging and a connection to their identity. In the face of generations of family separation, this powerful precedent will benefit Native children and communities for generations to come.

We are achieving things they told us were not possible. For decades, Washington's football team maintained and profited from a repulsive racial slur as its mascot and logo. When asked if they would ever change the team's name, then-owner Dan Snyder said, "Never," and every pollster told us to believe him. In 2020, standing on sixty-plus years of Native-led activism and organizing, we guided a coalition of forces that proved our critics wrong. Today, two-thirds of teams using "Native" mascots—over twenty-one hundred schools—have retired these racist names and images, a monumental victory for the well-being of our youth and for all of Indian Country.

Recent years have also seen historic levels of Native representation in the federal government. In 2018, Sharice Davids (Ho-Chunk Nation of Wisconsin) and Deb Haaland (Pueblo of Laguna) made history as the first Native American women elected to Congress. By 2020, they were among six Native lawmakers elected to the House of Representatives, a record-breaking number, and the following year Haaland was confirmed as secretary of the interior, making her the first Native woman in the presidential Cabinet. The moment that fifty-first vote came in, it felt like our world opened up with potential. It is because of those like Representative Davids, Secretary Haaland, and the leaders found on the following pages that Native youth can dream bigger and live a life of possibility. May they never be afraid of being the first Native person to do something.

The contributors to *My Life: Growing Up Native in America* are shining examples of our resilience and achievements. They also highlight a powerful truth about Native peoples across Turtle Island: our strength lies in our shared experience and in our diversity. We are Two-Spirit and LGBTQ+. We are Black, white, Latino, Muslim, Jewish, and so much more. We are artists and activists and athletes hailing from reservations and big cities and small towns. We perform drag. We create TV shows. We build game-changing businesses.

As we acknowledge and celebrate our historic progress, we are reminded that everything is done in community and collaboration and that our hard-fought victories come in partnership and solidarity with our allies. Our work alongside non-Natives not only advances the cause of equity and sovereignty for Native peoples; it also helps build a multiracial democracy and a healthy planet for generations to come.

We have seen the power of stories, and our dream for the essays and poems in this book is that they continue building empathy among our allies, generating strength and momentum through our shared values and shared experiences. May these pages heal and inspire you. May they serve as an invitation, a call to action, and a galvanizing force to join us in creating a better world for us all.

Iriwe Turahe (In a good way),
Crystal Echo Hawk (Pawnee)
Co-Founder and CEO, IllumiNative
2024

Our stories have the power to heal, both ourselves and the world around us.

—Alicia Elliott (Tuscarora)

LEMMING LESSONS

By Nasuġraq Rainey Hopson
(Iñupiaq)

I earned my first master's degree at age ten.

Of course, that is not what it looked like at the time. What it looked like was me being able to stuff twenty-five lemmings in the pockets of my bright blue windbreaker that was two sizes too big for me. But the pockets were large and easy to zip quickly—perfect for holding squirming rodents.

I caught all twenty-five lemmings in one afternoon. It wasn't particularly hard as I knew exactly where to find each one of them. I had spent the last month strategically arranging pieces of plywood stolen from my father's scrap pile across the tundra, focusing on places where the grass was thickest and the soil was dry, a lemming's preferred habitat.

The wood had to be the perfect size. Too big and the grass underneath would get compacted and hold too much water, making it damp and uninviting to the critters. Too small and the lemmings would not choose to make their fall time nests underneath them because it wouldn't offer enough protection. You had to trick the lemmings into thinking they had found the perfect hiding spots for nests and food stores: dry, safe, and easy to dig through. I waited and watched the weather, and when I judged it to be the right time, I walked along the well-known path and flipped each board over to reveal the startled little creatures. They would stay still just long enough for me to grab at them, their initial instinct to freeze, hoping camouflage would work in their favor, betraying them.

I spent years watching and catching and learning about lemmings. I guess most people would say that I was being a kid, that my boredom manifested itself into me being a bit wild. But I wasn't the only child chasing lemmings all summer and fall—there was a whole group of us who gravitated toward that type of stuff. And in an extremely rural and isolated arctic village in northern Alaska, there weren't that many options for fun. But it was more than just entertainment. We passed along knowledge to each other like good colleagues would, sharing information about locations and noting the

genetics in the slight differences in the markings on the lemmings' backs. We shared observations about how the population would grow and peak and then wane, and how this was
somehow tied to the number of predators. We figured out how
many lemmings owls would need to feed their young, and
we observed how lemmings treated their own young. Small
creatures have so many quiet lessons to teach us, though I've
often found that only children, who reside in the same type of
world, are open to them.

This is also where I learned about death.

A lemming I had caught leaped from the shoebox I was
holding them in (this was before I realized that jacket pockets were better). It fell beneath my feet, and I accidentally
stepped on it and killed it. They are such tiny, fragile creatures. I stared at the small bright spot of blood on its chin
and stood still as an unfamiliar feeling bloomed in me. It
was a mix of guilt and sadness and fear . . . and something
else. I wasn't yet old enough to understand that I could die,
that my friends and family could die, but in that moment, I
learned that I could cause death. I felt tiny suddenly, as every
single part of the world reached out to touch me gently. This
little death tied me to the world in such a permanent and
life-changing way. I was bound. I knew from then on that all
my actions would affect the world around me in ways I could

not understand and never would. But I became part of the world right then and there.

I took the lemming's body and buried it behind the house, fashioning a cross made of sticks that I placed over the grave. I didn't tell anyone about it.

The year after I caught twenty-five, I suddenly felt a little too old to be into lemmings, so I taught the younger kids what I knew in passing. My interests shifted to catching ground squirrels. They were harder to trap and a little bit scarier with their larger teeth and braver attitude. The next year it was songbirds, and the year after that, as I roamed farther away from my village and my world got bigger, the animals also got bigger and more varied. Soon I spent my time with aunts and uncles and cousins and mentors, roaming the tundra or beaches or ice floes, absorbing the world. But the pattern was the same, as I moved from earning one master's degree to the next. Binding myself with a thousand threads to the Arctic. To my Culture, to my People.

But this world, filled with animals and family and nature, wasn't the only world that existed.

Even as a child I knew when I crossed from one world into the next. When I was too little to know what to call this other world, I associated the boundary with a change in smells. When I walked into school, it smelled like the cleaner they used to shampoo the carpets, burnt coffee that Uncle said was weak and wouldn't even be worth drinking, and paint that was less than a year old. Smells with no depth, sterile and severe on the nose. Even the people who worked there matched the way the school smelled. The teachers there smelled like a base of nothing with a heavy splash of carefully choreographed personality of perfume or cologne or deodorant on top. The clinic smelled just like the school, as did some offices in the borough buildings too.

But me, I smelled like wolf fur on my parka and tundra sod in my nails. I smelled like seal oil from two nights ago somehow clinging to my skin. I smelled like Uncle's old cigarette smoke and the blue disinfectant we added to the indoor bucket to hide the fact that we had no flush toilets. I never knew how I smelled until I crossed that boundary into the other world. My world clung to me like my history, complicated and deep. I knew that these places in the other world, these places without normal smells, well, they hated me. They hated me in so many ways. They made fun of the way I spoke and the way I walked and the way I *thought*. These places scratched my skin with sneers and wrinkled noses. These places belittled me for my master's degrees. *Barbaric*, the walls would whisper. *Sad*, the clean floors would say to me. And the people there would mimic this disdain for me. *Uncivilized*, they said with the rolling of their eyes. I quickly learned at a young age how to navigate through this other clean, sterile, bland world. I rounded out my mouth, so my speech sounded like it fit. I changed my walk from the way I walk on ice and straightened my back, even though it made my calves ache. I read and read and read so I knew what kind of words to use. I coached my face to not move when they said things that stung like mosquito bites and avoided scratching the stings so they did not fester. Like the lemmings taught me, I worked to blend in when danger was around.

I did all these things to make it easier to be in that other world because my mother made it known that to be success-ful, I would have to be successful in *both* places. And I never gave it a second thought, because I was good at watching worlds and figuring all the wildlife out. Even if that wildlife included people from faraway places.

I earned my master's degree in the Western World at age seventeen.

One thing I gathered as I grew up was that there has been and always will be two separate worlds. They never mixed. Anything of my culture that made it into the school or clinic or borough buildings was scrubbed clean of its smell, too, scrubbed clean of the depth and character. And if it could not be made to fit and/or if it made the people who were there uncomfortable in any way, it was simply removed.

I got smart enough to graduate from high school and even got accepted to college in California. By then, my mother had left this world, taken by cancer. And the only real things she left behind were her wishes for me, like boards spread across the tundra in hopes that there would be bounty underneath, wishes for me to be successful in both worlds. So, I left all that was comfortable for me, left everything I knew, and stepped into the world that did not like the real me. But I did it carefully. I made sure to pack only clothes that did not look Indigenous. I only took a handful of pictures of family where you could not really tell from the background that I was from a small rural village in Alaska. I embraced vagueness as much as I could, making sure to scrub all the scents of home from my skin. When people asked where I was from, I smiled and did not answer if they asked only the once. I tucked that part of me into the folds so that I could avoid the disdain and noncelebration.

And, as you can imagine, I was miserable. You cannot deny parts of yourself, sever them from your daily life, and expect to be normal. I had gotten rid of all my anchors and was floating adrift. Lost. I was diagnosed with panic disorder and anxiety and found myself at weekly visits sitting across from a person who did his best to ignore where I came from, not once asking about the wounds growing in my Lemming Soul. *Best to focus on learning how to counter the attacks*, he would say, as he taught me breathing techniques. It made him uncomfortable that I was such a foreign entity, I think.

I learned the breathing techniques. Inhale, exhale, relax.

The second semester of my freshman year, I took an introduction to cultural anthropology course. It was required and it had openings, so I signed up, not really expecting much. The teacher was a woman originally from Australia; her accent came in and out as she spoke, like ocean waves. One day we opened the massively overpriced book and all of us turned to the page indicated. I was supposed to read the chapter ahead of time but hadn't, and I was surprised to see that half of the page was written about my own culture. The teacher briefly talked about the passage and asked if there were any questions. My palms started sweating almost immediately as I read my tribal name in black words on white paper again.

Iñupiaq.

I glanced around, wondering if anyone else saw my nervousness. A few students raised their hands to ask questions. The type of questions you ask if you want credit for participation. There was no anger, no disdain, no mocking laughter like I expected. Seeing my culture present in the other world pinned me to my desk. I felt like someone had taken a thumbtack and stuck it into my soul.

Here. You exist . . . here.

After class, I immediately made my way to the library. Seeing my culture in a book triggered something in me. I never imagined that someone would write anything about us in any book, and suddenly I wanted *more*. I wanted to see everything that was ever written about us. I found six books. Six. Four of them only had brief mentions of my culture and didn't go into any detail at all. Two of them were recountings of explorers, and each spent a couple chapters describing everything they saw and all of their experiences in our lands. Who they met. One of the books even included several black-and-white photos of Iñupiaq people. There was one of an Iñupiaq woman, her chin held high, eyes like flint, a slight smile on her lips. Three lines were tattooed on her chin, and she wore a caribou-skin atigi with beautiful qupak designs sewn into the hem. I could tell she would have never hidden anything of herself into the folds. I knew she would never be ashamed of where she was from. Of her history and family.

I felt those same tendrils of the world reach out to me as I did when that lemming died. I could feel myself being bound. But this time it was different. I knew without a doubt

I was on the way to something I could only vaguely see in the distance.

A couple days later, I hung back after my cultural anthropology class to talk with my teacher. She was one of the nicer people I had met, not overly friendly, but open and no-nonsense. She asked if she could help me.

"I'm Iñupiaq," I said, maybe a little too loudly. "I'm Iñupiaq from Alaska." I don't know what I expected to get from her by telling her this, but I was young and needed to move forward somehow. I needed to say those words out loud, in this place, this place that was thousands of miles from home. Her brow furrowed as she took a second to understand what I was saying, and then she smiled. "That's amazing," she said, and then proceeded to pepper me with questions. Each question was a gift. She truly was interested in my culture, each query insightful and encouraging. We sat outside the building and chatted for half an hour, and eventually she asked if I could do a presentation about my culture and the way I grew up. She offered in exchange pretty much a guaranteed A in the class. I accepted.

Books are powerful. Media is powerful. Movies and music and other expressions of human emotions and celebrations. Little did I know that this experience would lead me to a life creating as much media as I could that included our culture.

Our language, our history, our faces, and our stories. Eventually I would go on to make illustrations, documentaries, perfume, herbal remedies, videos, stickers, and anything else I could make, all with this one goal. Each thing I create, I create for that little girl catching lemmings in the tundra. Each thing I create is a love letter to her. Each thing I create is a means to celebrate childhood brilliance and culture. And when the negative voices creep into my head, when those voices of my childhood from the sterile place start scratching at my skin again, I remind them that I caught twenty-five lemmings in one day, and that they all fit in my pockets. And if I can do that, I pretty much could do anything.

ALL THE FALLING BABIES

By Eric Gansworth
(Onondaga)

If you've been raised in an Indian community, or at least in my Indian community, you know we only say "Native American" in mock seriousness, or in *serious* seriousness, for the benefit of one of those rare Indians who can't take a joke. If you're one of those rare Indians who can't take a joke, you're likely to receive some Side-Eyes from the Rest of Us. We suspect you're likely not from a community, even if we don't ask explicitly *what community claims you.* Though most Indians would not ask this, directly, it often lingers like stale cigarette smoke in a bingo hall.

But today, you might get asked this question. Your friend has lured you to this place with promises that you could smoke cigs without people and their prying eyes asking, *Is he smoking? Should we tell his mom?* Your friend says his Auntie is cool, that even though you're only fourteen, she won't care if you smoke. But as soon as you're in the door, you know this encounter with his auntie will make you squirm. The bad side of a community claiming you is that they know *all* your business. Especially if you're fourteen. She won't ask if you're smoking, but will she ask if a community claims you, or won't she ask? And will you know what you're supposed to say?

Your friend's flint-tongued, black-coffee-drinking, unfiltered-smoking Auntie *might* ask, because she's been asked. It's kind of the Rez Circle of Life. She was born on the Rez but raised in the city and came back to claim her family land on her own. You recognize her as soon as you step in the door and light your cig. You wouldn't have entered if you'd known who lived here. Enjoy that cig. You've crossed the threshold. It better be worth it.

This flint-tongued, black-coffee-drinking, unfiltered-smoking Auntie knows there are multiple ways to answer that question, *especially* for an Auntie like this. She's lived some of her childhood and most of her adult life on Dog Street, bisecting the Rez. Somebody could ask a member of her community if they claimed her. But say they ask someone she throat-punched in the second-grade Rez school lunchroom. That person might say, *Who? Never heard of her. Just must be a big old fake*, smiling, having waited all these years for that sweet revenge.

Lucky for you, that Auntie has been asked this question many times, so she might go easier on you. She didn't get this way overnight. She wants her community to claim her, but she knows some people had done custom Rez math and decided she wasn't Indian enough for the cutoff. What was her equation? Were there deductions for the second-grade throat-punch? She couldn't speak the language, plus she didn't do beadwork, plus she didn't even know how to Round Dance or Rabbit Dance.

No language
+ no beadwork
+ no dancing
Never find a man and have kids.

But she knows people lie. She got that flint tongue, biting the edges, so she wouldn't scream when people talked in front of her like she was invisible, a superpower that she never wanted. She pours you tar-black coffee and silently dares you to ask for milk and Equal to soften its bite. Then she offers you half-and-half and Sweet'N Low, but no Equal and no milk. "Sweet and Low is my Indian name," she says, laughing, then adds, "If you're a real Indian, milk is gonna trigger your lactose intolerance, so you might as well enjoy the richness of half-and-half before the pains set in. And no Indians ever get Equal, really, do they?" She does Rez math casually and fast all the time. And that's how you know she was raised in a community.

At fourteen, you've already learned to drink black coffee, so you *could* decline, but you might offend the Flint-Tongued Auntie if you don't accept her offer. Decisions, decisions. You know she has nieces and nephews, the real kind, the blood kind, who are not enrolled, so she might be eyeing you up to see if *you've* ever talked smack about *them* in the Rez school lunchroom with your own tongue you've been chipping the soft edges from. You're probably safe. You talk almost no smack in the lunchroom because you live in a Glass Long-house. No, not like some future Space Rez, everyone float-ing in zero gravity, after we've been shipped to the Moon, 'cause America has booted us out of our "ancestral territory" again, because it's run out of arable land *again*. No, your Glass Longhouse is metaphoric. (Using the word "metaphoric," even silently in your head, probably clicks you further into that "maybe no community claims you" territory. You smile to yourself because "territory" is a safe word.) You know at fourteen you have no room to smack-talk hardly anyone in the Rez school lunchroom.

You love all the interesting words in English and all the interesting words in Tuscarora, but you're running out of people to speak the interesting Tuscarora words to. The interesting words might be the only ones people remember, one day. We will loudly whisper to each other in Tuscarora while strolling around white people, so they worry we're talking about them. We might even forget that it's a verb-based language. When linguistics professors ask why we have a word for monkeys, we say it's because we can observe them and derive a name from their behavior. An animal doesn't have to be Indigenous for us to give it a name. Except, already, at fourteen, you can't remember if the word for monkey translates to "it hangs from its long tail" or "it throws its own shit at you." One of these definitions is more useful than the other.

Her name might be Delores or Denise or Deanna or Diana, you didn't quite catch it when you walked in, and your friend just calls her *Auntie D*. But you know she's not a Dorothy, or Doris, or a Dot, like your own Auntie, or maybe she is and she's made up a younger name to suit her sense of style. You start thinking of her as Flinty D, and you hope your brain is not also like a Glass Longhouse, 'cause if it is, you know she's going to peek.

"Oh, I know you. You're the Superhero," Flinty D says, rapping her knuckles hard on her gleaming Formica table, with the million glints of embedded glitter stabbing your eyes. You realize the name Formica means "a Substitution *For Mica*" (or "Fake Mica" if you're being truthful). Is it good or bad that she's pegged you as the kid everyone called Batman ("Bats" for short)? It started when you were three, loving that TV show maybe too vigorously. You calmed down a few years ago, but your love of Batman is what adults remember about you.

"Folks think you want to be a hero, rescuing everyone," she adds. "Hah! I think you just want to run around the city with your underpants on the outside to show off the goods." Her comment reminds you that her tongue should be registered as a deadly weapon. She's of course right that you are enjoying the discoveries of puberty, all the new ways you're growing, but nobody wants to be called out for that. So being bold in the beginnings of your man-body, you try to suggest she's past her prime.

"Only old people call me that, these days," you say. It is an unwise move. Despite your bold new body, she knows the weaknesses of all the superheroes. It's her job. She knows she's lived a divided life and sometimes it's her job to be a supervillain. Maybe she's your Catwoman.

"Elders? Is that who you mean?" Flinty D asks, hinting that you've forgotten you're Indian. The word "Elders" hasn't caught on, but respecting your older community members is an expectation firmly in place. The families who cave to using nursing homes get Side-Eyes for losing their way, as if the rest of us could know their circumstances. "We're called Elders 'cause we have the wisdom of a lived life, and we're offering it, so you don't have to suffer the same pains, the same aches? And today's your lucky day, Superhero. I have some Wisdom for you."

You don't express whether you'd like or dislike her offer, because Flinty D is absolutely going to share her Elder Wisdom. "If you want to keep being the Superhero, you're probably planning to pack your bags, leave the Rez, and head to the city." She pauses and smiles, and slides your coffee close, so you can see your reflection in its dark mirror. "You didn't say how you wanted it, sweetened and lightened?" she asks, pointing with her lips to my cup.

"It's fine this way," you say. "Don't waste your resources."

"So courteous! You waste money your mom don't have on them funny books," she says, sliding your cup closer to you, letting you know that you'd better not waste the cup she's poured.

"I don't think twenty-five cents is gonna break her," you say, quoting the average comic book price. Until recently, you had no after-school job and you didn't know that every quar-ter she gave you for comics came from somewhere else. Your family doesn't have a rainy-day fund. Every time it rains, you dig out coffee cans to catch the ceiling drips and your mom washes her hair in the gathered water, saying rainwater is the purest, ignoring that it has been filtered through the rotting roof of your house. Turning leaks into luxury is your mother's superpower.

"Kids never think of the value," Flinty D says. "They all think we're Plastic Man or Elastic Woman and that we can stretch anything for as long as we need it. That we could take a meal we set for three and make it so unexpected relatives who show up exactly at dinnertime can have a plate. That's why superheroes are for kids. When you grow up, you know every rubber band breaks if you yank too hard. When you grow up, you'll know who has that little extra in the serv-ing bowl come dinnertime. Who you might suddenly decide to drop in on. You'll know who all the Elastic Women are. Maybe you'll also learn not to stretch them."

You could say your family shelled out way more for your brother's lacrosse equipment than they ever would for your comics. You could have long, long runs of both Marvel and DC for the cost of one lacrosse stick or jersey. Your mom says lacrosse is your closest brother's only chance. (*For what?* you think.) You wonder what your chances are. You can't throw or catch or even cradle the ball competently. You can't participate in your community pastime. You could blame your eyes, which aren't quite aligned right, but everyone knows you've committed the cardinal sin. You don't care about lacrosse and never did. You could list all the reasons, but they won't matter. You'll never be a community star, giving people hope, holding that MVP trophy.

"So why would I have to leave the Rez to be a superhero?" you ask, knowing you're going to get there at some point, so you cut to the chase. At this moment, you are more like Batman than ever, dangling among the tops of skyscrapers, by the thinnest of ropes.

"You tell me." She turns your way. "Seem I heard everyone thinks you're Mister Smarty-Pants. You read all the funny books and you done your calculations. Where do the heroes live?"

You don't mention that when you and your classmates all got shipped to the white middle school off the Rez, your new teachers didn't believe *any* Indians were among the smartest kids in the school. One suggested that maybe you were just *smart for an Indian*. You are smart enough to know you're never going to change that teacher's mind. But as you try to hide that teacher's voice deep in the Glass Longhouses of your Heart and Mind, you consider Flinty D's question.

DC heroes live in fake places like Gotham City, Metropolis, Star City, Capitol City, and Central City, and Marvel heroes mostly live in New York City, like you might run into Ben Grimm or Spider-Man on the street if you ever got to Manhattan.

"All the time, superheroes rescue babies falling from tall, tall buildings. Villains know the buildings to go after," Flinty D says. "All the babies falling from so many tall buildings."

"We don't have buildings that tall out here," you say. The Rez continues to fill with trailers. Even frame houses with more than one story rarely have attics. Your mom says attics are for packrats who have extra stuff they don't need. "Most of us don't even have a second story," you observe, noting the stairway behind Flinty D, hidden behind a curtain. "But you do."

"Don't you worry about me, Bats. I got plenty of stories." She laughs at her own wordplay. She could develop a new word for monkey. "But we're talking about you. Babies are the most precious accessory for superheroes. Those heroes like their sexy outfits and wrestling other weirdos in other sexy outfits, but at some point, to be true heroes, they gotta arrive just in time for those babies. So many, many falling babies you'd think they were apples past harvest. But look careful at your funny books. All the falling babies are white. They're not like fruit. When an apple falls, it's left for bees and deer to eat. Damaged goods. No one wants a bruised apple." At some point, Flinty D's been called an Apple, and she's prepping you for the same fate.

Would you concede that cities were complicated, had greater needs? Wasn't the need great enough on a Rez to keep a superhero busy? Rez babies deserved to be caught. Even if the fall was from a one-story window, where they get a bruise or two, the way you yourself toppled out your own home's window before you'd learned how to break your fall.

"When the villain came for our babies and snatched them, to brainwash them into becoming someone else, to forget their origins, no hero showed up to rescue them," she says, offering you a cig from her unfiltereds pack on the Formica table, but you pass, knowing she'll keep track and one day come back to collect all you owe. "And the villain? Why, the villain turned out to be the United States, itself. And they were so clever, they called the brainwashing instrument a school, so parents thought it was a good thing."

You know she's speaking the truth. When three of your four grandparents were taken to the Indian boarding schools as little kids, that theft was indeed perpetrated by agents of the United States, "for their own good." No superhero snatched them from the departing train, to deliver them back into the arms of weeping parents, and no American hero ever would. You realize Superman's colors are close to the flag's. Wonder Woman and Captain America literally wear versions of the flag as their costumes—truth in advertising on their exposed underpants showing off the abundant goods.

"I'm smart enough to know there's no such thing as superheroes," you say. "I just like to draw them and read about them."

"I didn't say there's no such thing. You don't know, we have our own heroes. You could draw them and their stories," Flinty D says, and then pauses. Somehow she also knows you draw. "But I bet you don't know who Flint and Sapling are, the Bad Mind and the Good. I bet your grandparents got shipped away before they heard about those heroes who shaped our world."

You don't have any idea who she's talking about, but you're too afraid to admit that her sharp tongue is the only Flint you've encountered.

"Without knowing they had Indian heroes to rescue them, your grandparents had to discover their own powers as they tumbled toward home. They learned how to make it back to the Rez on their own. Sometimes you don't need to be super. Sometimes being a plain old hero is good enough to do the job."

"And how do you know all this?" you ask, trying to peer

inside the Glass Longhouses of Flinty D's Heart and Mind, to see if you can catch a glimpse of these heroes she mentions. "How do you know what it takes to become a hero?"

"Don't bother trying your x-ray vision," she laughs. "My kryptonite is well-hidden." But you already know her kryptonite. It is that eternal Indian question: *What community claims you?* You wonder if she regrets the secret origin of unwisely landing a throat-punch on the wrong kid in the Rez school lunchroom. If she could travel through time, would she take back the punch or did it feel too good to take back? "I know all this 'cause I was just like you," Flinty D says, "thinking I could dress in my sexy duds and save the day."

"So what happened?" you ask. You can't see into the Glass Longhouses of her Heart and of Mind, but you know her parents took her away "for her own good," believing the Boarding School idea, rising from dormancy, like all the strongest supervillain plans. You know she came back on her own, because she's telling you right now. You know community members sometimes still blame her for her history just the same. You know she hates the power of invisibility, understanding that superpowers are sometimes a curse, instead of a gift.

"I'd like to say that the white world wants only white heroes," she says, draining her cup of tar-black coffee as if she'd doctored it up. "That heroes wear masks so no one can tell who's under that wild and secret face. It would be a good story, if I got rejected by people in need."

"You'd *like* to say that, but you can't?" you ask. Does a hero only exist if there are people to save, villains to conquer, babies to catch? "Is that why you came back to the Rez and gave up on being a hero? Too much rejection?"

"You think being enrolled is so easy, Bats, 'cause you got your red card, and your enrollment number on Nation Stationery, but you're close enough to growing up that you're soon gonna know what it really means to draw that line, to know where you fall." Flinty D looks at the carbon flakes in her pie-tin ashtray like she's glancing at your future. "But at some point, someone you love is not gonna be enrolled, and you're gonna have to decide if it's still so cut-and-dry to claim and be claimed. And just to be clear, I said *you* would probably head to the city, showing off your new superhero muscles, seeking out people to rescue," she reminds you. "Someone's gonna ask you and demand an answer. It's hard. But me? I didn't give up."

"Well, what happened to you, then?"

"I learned the same hard lessons your grandparents did. What do you think I'm doing right now?" And as she says it, you feel heat rise on your face, the scorch of embarrassment. "I'm saving the falling babies, rescuing them even as we speak, with the powers I have. Like any other superhero, I have claimed my place." You discover at that moment you're on the top floor of your own burning building of pride and you're going to topple any moment. The friend you walked in here with is nowhere to be found. It is only you and the roof and the flames.

"Bats, can't you feel my arms reaching out, getting ready to wrap around you?" she says, showing her open palms.

And all at once, you do, and you reach across the table, grasp that outstretched hand. You know what community claims you, suddenly understanding that you have just been rescued.

KUTÂPUTUSH, KUTÂPUTUSH

By Kara Roselle Smith
(Chappaquiddick Wampanoag)

Before I learned how to mend my own heart, I learned how
  to break it.
And before I saw the damage in my own, I saw it first in my
  mother's,
Who inherited it from her mother, who inherited it from hers,
  and hers, and hers, and hers, and hers.
An ancestral line wrought with an agony so deep, buried for
  generations.

But an ancestral line tethered with a will so strong it could be
  felt for generations to come.

Before I felt its pull
I always wanted to be somewhere else,
Someone else.

I knew just what to do to make my heart ache.

Comparison my sustenance,
gambling on unavailability my vice.
No matter the pain that followed,
There was nothing quite like the habitual high of breaking
my own heart.

I didn't recognize the wound
That caused me to seek out this pain
Until I saw it in my mother.

I saw her heart cry.
Mourning time lost.
Mourning the sacrifices.
Mourning the ridicule for attempts made to break the cycle,
directed toward both her and her mother.
Mourning the opportunity that I wasn't seizing.

It was then that I saw the women before me.
And in them I saw myself.

Kutâputush kin, for granting my existence and for your never-
ending perseverance.
A people whose power was forever doubted,
the same doubt that found its way to me,
but a doubt then unwoven by my very existence.

Kutâputush earth, for letting me land.
Kutâputush air, for teaching me to be nimble.
Kutâputush fire, for teaching me how to trailblaze.
And Kutâputush water, for teaching me that I cannot be con-
tained.

A friend looks over to me and says,
"I like your eyes."
"Thanks, I got them from my mother."

Kutâputush, Ma, for your eyes.
For allowing me to see.

A gift to me
And the seven generations to come.

We are enrolled members of tribes and dis-
enrolled members, ineligible members and
tribal council members. We are full-blood,
half-breed, quadroon, eighths, sixteenths,
thirty-seconds. Undoable math. Insignifi-
cant remainders.

—Tommy Orange (Cheyenne, Arapaho)

BEING INDIAN

By Kimberly Guerrero
(Colville, Salish-Kootenai)

It's 1971. I'm four years old and I've got dreams. Big dreams. I want to sail around the world as Jacques Cousteau's assistant, give birth to at least two litters of kittens, and join the Jackson Five. But my biggest dream, the one that burns deepest in my bones fueling my wildly overactive imagination, is this: I want to be Indian. I want the horses and teepees, the songs and dances, the laughter and stories. I wanna live life on the move, going on adventures with my family and friends, being in nature all day, every day—all while wearing buckskin leggings and moccasins, a war shirt, and a feather in my hair.

I learn about Indians every chance I get. My mom gets me these picture books from the Stuckey's rest stop that show all the different tribes across America. I memorize which books on the encyclopedia shelf at the top of the stairs have pictures of Indians. I glue myself to the television looking for shows with Indians. Real Indians, I mean. I don't for one second buy that the bad guys on horses with their goofy face paint, bad wigs, and crayon-colored feathers are Indians. Nope. Especially not the cartoon one who hunts Bugs Bunny. One day, I'm eating cereal sprawled out in front of the tube when *The Brady Bunch* comes on. The Bradys are visiting the Grand Canyon when Bobby and Cindy spot an Indian boy, Jimmy, and get lost in the canyon trying to find him. I'm out-of-my-gourd excited until I discover that Jimmy has run away from home because he wants to be an astronaut and is afraid that his grandfather, who practices the old ways, won't let him. I wanna jump through the screen, shake the kid by the shoulders, and scream, "Jimmy, what are you thinking?! Your grandfather will understand—he's an Indian Chief for crying out loud! GO. HOME."

Then one afternoon, my mom and dad ask me to come upstairs with them to my bedroom. *Crap.* I scramble, thinking of all the things I know I've done wrong or may have done wrong in the past couple of weeks. Whatever it is it must be bad because my dad, who's normally a Chatty Cathy, gets suspiciously quiet and all red in the face—like he's holding in a mountain of toots. My mom sits me down on my bed and with the precision of a special ops bomb disposal specialist drops this piece of life-altering news:

I am adopted.

Time freezes. The beat of my heart takes on this slow, deafening *BOOM-BOOM. BOOM-BOOM.* The inner dialogue that ceaselessly rages between my ears gets really small and quiet and goes something like this: *I mean, yeah. Okay. I do look totally different than them. When we go to the lake, they come back red, I come back brown. We don't really seem to be into the same things—they don't like nature as much as I do and don't seem able to talk to animals or trees like I can. And whenever I watch that singing game on* Sesame Street*—"One of these things is not like the others, one of these things doesn't belong"—I feel like vomiting. Right. I'm adopted. CRAP! If these people got me, that means they can give me back! I'm not sure where back is, but I damn sure know it's not good. But then . . . I'm* not *good. I know what I am; deep down I've always known: a mistake. Some sub-human species that has slithered out of a hellhole and is faking my way through.* I don't belong.

Just as I feel myself surrendering to what I can only hope is a merciful bout of spontaneous sub-human combustion, my mom brings out this thick orange book. On the front cover of this book is a drawing of horses, teepees . . . and Indians.

She carefully opens it, points to an old black-and-white photograph, and says, "See him? That is your great-grandfather."

People . . . it is an Indian Chief. An Indian Chief sitting on a horse wearing this epic for-real feather headdress and exuding a degree of badassery that quite frankly scares the bejesus out of me. Mom then turns the page to show me a picture of a beautiful, familiarly chubby-cheeked girl in a buckskin dress. "And this is your great-grandmother." She reads me what's written below the photo. The girl is married to my great-grandfather, and it says that she herself is a descendant of a Chief named Seattle.

Next thing I know, I'm sitting in the bathroom, all quiet and alone. I'll think about the whole adoption thing later, but right now all I can do is stare at my face in the mirror. My Indian face. Dreaming about being Indian is one thing. But actually *being* Indian? What does that mean? What do you do when a dream this big comes true? It'll take me a whole lifetime to fully answer that question, but even in that moment I know that being Indian, really being Indian, is something way bigger than horses and teepees and feathers in your hair.

Once this reality sets in, I begin seeing Indians *everywhere*. At church, we sit in front of Coach Kaniatobe and his family. His dad's a big, gentle man who makes this incredible "stuff." If you rub it on sprains, bruises, finger jams, and the like, I kid you not, you're better the next day. Rumor has it that Mr. Kaniatobe makes it for the Dallas Cowboys. (One day, when I'm in college, I will sit in front of our star quarterback, who will go on to become the Dallas Cowboys' star quarterback. I will turn around and tell him I'm from Oklahoma, too, and find out that Coach Kaniatobe was his high school coach!) On the pew in front of us sits my future softball coach, Miss Fuller, and her brother, Curtis. Next to them sits their sweet momma who grew up on a real live reservation in South Dakota. Even though she is missing the bottom half of one of her arms, she beads me the most beautiful hair ties and necklaces. There are also Indian kids on my (not adopted) brother's little league team and Indian people who work at the bank and at the Piggy Wiggly and, eventually, I'll start school and make all kinds of Indian friends. Some outgoing and goofy like me (my friend Vicky Billy and I are so much alike, people will mistake us for twins) and some shy and quiet like David Williston (our senior year of high school, I'll ask David to be my escort on the Football Homecoming court and he'll simply duck his head, smile, and nod). I realize pretty quickly that the whole horses and teepees thing—which, don't get me wrong, is still crazy awesome—is just the tip of the iceberg.

A couple months after I learn that I'm Indian (and adopted, but honestly, I still don't want to think about that), my mom drives me to a Choctaw camp up in the mountains where folks are learning to sing old songs and dance old dances they've just brought back from Mississippi. Even though the ladies invite my mom into the camp, she waits outside in the station wagon and reads a book. They take me into the circle, and I see more Indians gathered in one place than I have ever seen in my whole life. It's incredibly cool, but I know I don't fit in. I feel like a dirty turnip in a candy dish. Crap. Now that stupid *Sesame Street* song's playing in my head. But the Indian people, they treat me just like I'm one of them! Which, technically speaking, I guess I am . . . ? Even though it's ungodly hot and buggy and I have to dance this one dance holding hands with this giant kid with sweaty palms, I cannot believe my luck—I am dancing real Indian dances with real Indians.

For weeks, we practice for the opening night of the very first Kiamichi Owa-Chito Festival up in our state park. It's a big deal. All the campsites are full, and the park is crawling with people. But about a half hour before we're supposed to dance, it starts clouding up. A giant bolt of lightning cracks open the sky, followed by this terrifying boom of thunder. Raindrops start hitting the ground like projectiles from heaven. I love thunderstorms, but this one isn't like any I've ever seen. This storm is like a person. Like it's shouting and crying and laughing all at the same time, trying to get our attention. It shakes the trees, the rocks, the river, and us as we stand there under an awning in our beautiful regalia. I feel a good cry coming on, sad that we all worked so hard and don't get to show everyone the dances. But then, as I watch the storm rage on, something about *not* dancing feels right. Almost like the dances we were supposed to dance had already been danced. A little while later, we quietly pack up and drive home.

A few months later, on a bitterly cold, gray Sunday afternoon in December, my dad asks me if I want to drive out with him to Goodland. I'm not exactly sure what Goodland is, but as I am always up for a road trip, I jump in the front seat of the station wagon as Dad loads the back with boxes of Wranglers and winter coats from his dry goods store in town. I ask what we're doing, and he says dropping off some stuff for Christmas. *For who?* I wonder.

After about an hour, we pull off the two-lane highway and drive into a little grass square surrounded by a handful of small, old buildings. We park in front of a simple wooden house, and I notice there are a few other houses around the square that look exactly like it, which for some reason makes me feel icky. No, more than icky. Scared. On the front porch of each house, kids are hanging out. The more I look at them, the more I realize that these kids look just like me. Older, but just like me. These kids are Indian. Dad asks me if I want to come in. I shake my head and slink down in the seat. I peek over the dashboard to watch them, their breath filling the cold air like smoke. Some look bored. Others are roughhousing— just kids being kids. But there's something different about them. Something that makes my heart hurt. When Dad gets back in the station wagon, I ask him if these kids go to school here. He says, no, they live here. It's an orphanage. My world stops. I can't breathe. *They're orphans*, I think. *Like me. But not like me.* As Dad drives away, I look back. I can't stop looking. Part of me feels like I should make him stop the car and take me back to stay there with them. The other part of me is like, *Are you crazy? Turn the heck around and keep your mouth shut.* I turn around. On the long drive home, I feel an unbearable load of guilt piling onto the shame that already burns in the core of my being like a nuclear reactor. Those kids, the memory of them, will stay with me forever.

I have them with me that next summer when my mom, big brother, and I hop into a baby-blue conversion van with my antique-dealer grandparents and drive all the way from Oklahoma to an antique show in Seattle. After a visit to the top of the Space Needle, my mom walks me over to the statue of Chief Seattle and gives me—gives us—our space. I feel small and shy as I approach the still, bronze figure. I stand there studying his face, looking at his arm stretched out over my head. It feels like an invisible hand is squeezing my heart. In a whisper, and trying to do it without moving my lips so no one can see, I introduce myself. I tell him I have to talk to him. I have questions. A lot of them. About me. About the orphans. About what being Indian means. After a while, the constant chatter in my head stops, and I hear answers. A lot of them. Answers that not only help the shame and guilt feel a little less heavy; they also gift me with two other things— direction and purpose.

A few years later, I'll trade in the dream of becoming a cat-bearing oceanographer/pop star for the dream of becoming an actress. I'll eventually find out that the odds of pulling this off as a brown girl in Hollywood during those days are only slightly better than the odds of birthing kittens. I'll head out to LA and attend a college so big that everyone in my entire hometown could fit into one section of our football stadium. A Kiowa-Delaware professor will take me under his wing and introduce me to Indians in LA, San Francisco, and New York. I'll meet iconic activists, actors, singers, dancers, artists, writers, and Native folks from all walks of life—many of whom will become like family to me. My tribe.

Speaking of family and tribe, when I'm twenty I will find my biological family. I will watch my birth parents wrap my adopted parents in blankets, and we'll all dance around the circle at Cherokee Holidays. And up on my grandfather's reservation, he and my uncle will take me before our tribal council. Right before we go in, I'll suffer a panic attack after convincing myself that the council is going to kick me out of the tribe. Instead, they will lovingly wrap me in a blanket and tell me that our people, like the salmon, always know how to find their way home.

Those answers I heard on that drizzly day in Seattle, whether real or imagined, will lead me to spend a large part of my life traveling to different tribal communities where I'll make more friends-like-family, and my "tribe" will grow. I will pour my heart into Native kids from around the country, eventually helping them learn how to tell their own stories through filmmaking. Back in Hollywood, I'll stay in the trenches alongside my storytelling tribe, fighting that exact same fight—to be able to tell our own stories in our own way. Years upon years will pass, and there will be times when I don't think we'll ever live to see the breakthrough.

But then, one day, things will change.

One day, I'll even get to pull on a pair of fringed buckskin leggings, a war shirt, and the most beautiful pair of beaded moccasins—all of it made with love and care by Indian hands. I will sit on my horse with a feather in my hair surrounded by horses and teepees, songs and dances, laughter and stories, as I join my family and friends on a great adventure. A story-telling adventure. And even though cameras will be rolling, what we feel won't start with the word "action" or end with the word "cut." It will feel bigger than that. It will feel like an old wound healing. It will feel like an orphan finding home. It will feel like a sacred belonging. It will feel like being Indian.

GROWING UP PUEBLO (AND WHITE) IN AMERICA

By Somáh Toya Haaland
(Laguna, Pueblo)

Growing up Pueblo
and White

means
my privilege shifts
in each space I occupy

my code switch is always on
for emotional safety

I can simultaneously be
both the oppressed
and the oppressor

means

my relatives are

cowboys

and Indians

and both

and neither

means

I am still subject to

the American project of assimilation

it has only been three generations

since my ancestors were taken

to St. Catherine's as children

I grew up thinking this was

a normal part of our history

until Intro to Native American Studies

sophomore year I learned how lucky I was

that they came home from that school at all

means

I grew up despising the shape of

my chin my cheeks my dimples

but when my grandmother left earthside
I began to see her
in my own reflection

my features have always been Pueblo
the only reason I thought I didn't want them
was because White Supremacy told me
they were unattractive

means
I have been to more funerals than
most of my non-Native friends and
I have to listen to them say they relate
when they will never fully understand
I'm not just grieving my relatives but
every single bit of knowledge lost
when so much
has already been stolen

when I go to visit their resting places
tribal police stop to ask if I'm a member
I have to say
"No

but I grew up in that trailer
with the red porch
right across the way
I am Mary Toya's grandchild"

I promise that I belong here
even though I don't have a card
to prove it

means
I can tell a White person that I am Native
and they will respond with something racist
straight to my face because
in their mind
they have already killed the Indian
and saved nothing

They only see the parts of me
that they can understand

when someone tells me
that I am the first Native person they have met
in the same sentence as
"but you couldn't play Native on TV"

the only response I can muster is
"I know"

I over-explain
put a disclaimer on my existence
when I'll never be in control
of how I am perceived
anyway

There is this recurring sharpness in my gut
familiar since a White man
came to my Albuquerque preschool
to teach us about the Pueblos
like I wasn't still living at one
just forty miles away

he had brought a little manta
probably the same size
as the one I had at home
and let a blond girl in my class
try it on like a costume

a piercing twinge
the urge to raise my hand

to stand up and say something
to break out of the seemingly
invisible box that I am stuck in
and shout

I'm right here.
We still exist.

But that sharpness is echoed by
the ringing in my chest
the racing heart
every time I hope to be seen
with relatives I haven't met yet

When I sat down to write about
Growing Up Native in America
I thought
am I Native enough
to take up space
on these pages?

I have never known
how much energy to occupy

in the rooms full of people
who I relate to the most

At an AISES conference in high school
I introduced myself to a room full of kids
and said I was from Laguna
one came to find me after
he said something to me in Keres
just to see if I knew how to respond
"at least she can speak" he said
I know what I look like
to people who don't know me
so
I was proud that I passed his test

When I go to Jemez to dance
I am always ready to explain
who I am
who my family is
that I grew up mostly at Laguna
so I don't speak Towa
and I'm sorry that
I don't understand

everything
but I am listening

I know that
I will be recognized
if I continue to show up

When I was little
my family always called me
Wooly because
I am the only one
with thick, wavy, brown hair
a trait which must have come
from the same person
whose name is absent
from my birth certificate

But one thing about being Native is
we often carry many names

duhinume tsiyaa'dyu'mai shuwimi hanu
my name is To Get Close, and I am turquoise clan

I wonder if I was given this name

so I would remember
to examine things
a little more carefully

to invite a shift
in perspective

      I am either Ka'waikameh
             or I am not

So why did I grow up
constantly being made
to measure my belonging?

I know this much is true:

being Pueblo means
the only currencies
that have any value to me
are love and reciprocity

being Pueblo means
I know how to belly laugh

in the thick of mourning
because the rest of us
are still here, together

being Pueblo means
my love for the Earth
is not a trend or a choice
but a practice and an obligation
that I have inherited
from beyond more generations
than I can count

I am still learning
which parts of my judgment
have not been blighted
by Whiteness
by the standard I am held to
in every space that doesn't fully see me

It is sometimes tricky finding
balance
on this tightrope of privilege
but I have plenty of
friends siblings aunties kin

to help me up
when I lose it

We grow up playing in the dirt
running from rattlesnakes
climbing rocks and skinning knees
so I am not afraid of falling

Being Native in "America"
is more than a blood quantum
it is a state of mind

and I've never met a rez dog
who wasn't mixed.

THE BULLSEYE
AND THE BIRD'S EYE

By Angeline Boulley
(Sault Ste. Marie Tribe of Chippewa Indians)

Dear Reader,

Identity is a familiar theme in my writing. My stories focus on Native teens claiming their identities and finding their places in the world, while also solving mysteries and falling in love. When I was growing up, my Ojibwe identity was challenged rather than validated. It messed with my sense of worth well into adulthood.

I used to visualize Native identity like an archery target—a series of concentric circles, with each ring symbolizing a definition of "being Native." The largest ring had the most inclusive definition and held everyone who claimed Native heritage. Inside that was a slightly smaller ring filled with those who knew which tribal Nation they were descended from; i.e., they claimed a connection to a specific Native Nation. Nested within that was a smaller ring for those whose specific tribe or band also claimed them as an enrolled member. The smaller the ring, the more narrow the definition of Native identity. The bullseye in the center, therefore, had the most exclusive definition. I believed there were Native people, a small group of fortunate individuals, whose identity was universally accepted by everyone. I also realized that there was a difference between where I might place myself within the archery target and where others would fix my position.

It's no surprise that Daunis, the protagonist in my debut novel, *Firekeeper's Daughter*, would share these same struggles. She and I are both light-skinned Ojibwe women with a Native dad, a non-Native mom, and a maternal grandmother who did not care at all for Native Americans. We both experienced white peers asking, *What are you?* White adults phrased the identity question as, *Where does your family come from?* My response was met with a version of, *Really? You don't look Native.* Most white people saw Native identity as a binary—either you were Native or you weren't—and their definition of "Native" was limited to uninformed stereotypes. Since I didn't look like the Indian maiden on the Land O'Lakes butter package, my claim of being Ojibwe did not compute. The interaction was often followed by, *Yeah, but at least you're not like those* other *Indians.* This was intended as a compliment to me, that I didn't fit the negative image they had about Native Americans.

Early on, Daunis and I learned that others saw us differently than we saw ourselves. In chapter 1, Daunis shares a memory illustrating the push and pull of her Anishinaabe (Native) and Zhaaganaash (non-Native) grandmothers on her identity:

> When I was seven, I spent a weekend at Gramma Pearl's tar-paper house on Sugar Island. I woke up crying with an earache, but the ferry to the mainland had shut down for the night. She had me pee in a cup, and poured it into my ear as I rested my head in her lap. Back home for Sunday dinner at GrandMary and Grandpa Lorenzo's, I excitedly shared how smart my other grandmother was. *Gramma Pearl fixed my earache with my pee!* GrandMary recoiled and, a heartbeat later, glared at my mother as if this was her fault. Something split inside me when I saw my mother's embarrassment. I learned there were times when I was expected to be a Fontaine and other times when it was safe to be a Firekeeper.

This cornerstone moment changes how Daunis views herself. She will spend the rest of her childhood and adolescence amplifying or de-emphasizing aspects of her identity to blend more successfully with whichever side of the family she is with. In fact, Daunis will become so adept at this code switching that she will create different behaviors or rules for other aspects of her identity, such as Hockey World and Science World. Her self-construct is a mercurial target, the bullseye constantly shifting in response to the people around her.

My own cornerstone moment also involved a maternal grandmother. Grandma Bea was proud of her English and Norwegian heritage. She told me it was a good thing that I had inherited my skin color from her side of the family, otherwise I might have been as dark as my father. I was puzzled by the remark. My dad was my hero—a well-read, kind, muscular man, with russet-brown skin showing barely visible tattoos from his Navy days. My ivory skin was a lucky break, according to Grandma Bea, and I had better avoid the sun. She wasn't concerned about wrinkles or skin cancer, just the melanin-triggered prejudices she espoused. To my grandmother, Native identity was defined by skin color.

In college, I learned that Native identity was defined by where I lived. There was a local Native tribe a mere three miles from the university I attended. (It may as well have been three hundred miles away, for the lack of Native students on campus.) I was asked to serve on a diversity committee within the School of Education. Since I was the president of the American Indian Student Organization on campus, it wasn't an unusual request. What was out of the ordinary was when the committee chairperson, a faculty member who was non-Native, asked me to recommend a different individual to represent the Native student body, preferably a male (to help balance out the primarily female committee) and someone from the nearby reservation. The implication was clear: I wasn't Native enough because I wasn't from the local tribal community. I felt embarrassed about being asked to find a replacement. It didn't matter that there were eleven other Native tribes in Michigan, including mine. Nor did it matter that the vast majority of Native Americans do not grow up on reservations. To the diversity committee chair, the bullseye of the identity target was filled with Native Americans from the local community. The rest of us landed in one of the outer rings of the target. (By the way, I was invited back when the young man I recommended was a no-show for the committee meetings. I declined.)

After graduating from college, I was hired by the local Indian tribe, and I learned that Native identity—to some—was defined by Indian blood quantum, or IBQ. There are 574 federally recognized Indian tribes, each with the sovereign right to determine the eligibility requirements for citizenship. The majority of federally recognized tribes include an IBQ requirement. The most common minimum requirement is 1/4 IBQ, which means that one of your four grandparents must be traced to the official tribal rolls or historical documents listing those who were part of the distinct Native community. To those who cling to IBQ, the identity target has a bullseye labeled "full bloods," and each circle rippling outward has a decreasing IBQ minimum: 3/4, 1/2, 1/4, 1/8. My own tribe uses lineal descendancy rather than a minimum IBQ. This means children are enrolled because their family tree connects them to ancestors on the tribal rolls, regardless of how many generations between the child and the ancestor.

My job with the local tribe was to be an advocate for the Native students attending the public middle school. I was to help those students who, as enrolled tribal members, were eligible for the advocacy services. There were students, however, who were not eligible but still considered themselves Native. I helped them regardless, because I already knew from personal experience that enrollment and eligibility for services was a complicated matter.

Although my tribe did not calculate IBQ for enrollment purposes, they still included the documentation for other purposes. For example, there were scholarships and, in Michigan, a tuition waiver that did require a minimum Indian blood quantum. My own IBQ, unofficially, was 1/2 because two of my four biological grandparents are Native. But my father was born at home on Sugar Island and didn't have a birth certificate until he wanted to join the Navy. His biological father, who was also Ojibwe, wasn't listed on his birth certificate for unspecified reasons. The result is that my dad's IBQ is calculated only from his mother's side. Officially, I am listed as 1/4 IBQ. I know from my family history that IBQ can differ significantly from what is "official" or documented and what is "unofficial" or the real story. Because of my personal experience, I was determined to help all Native kids as their designated Student Advocate. I never wanted to invalidate a Native student's identity by gatekeeping services from them. I decided that my career in Indian education would be spent increasing access and services. My true purpose was to support Native children and teens as they formed their own self-construct.

There are some Native people with a negative, even hostile, opinion of lineal descendancy tribes such as mine. I have worked for other tribes whose community members did not think highly of my tribe, which is the largest federally recognized tribe east of the Mississippi River. My individual IBQ meant nothing to the disgruntled co-worker who once told me to go work for my own "washed-out" tribe. An Indian Health Service (IHS) worker at another tribe's clinic once complained about having to provide health care services to my tribe's "barely Native" members when their own tribe's descendants, unenrolled children or grandchildren, were not eligible to receive care. Even friends from these other tribes would joke about me being "the best of the worst" tribe. This lateral targeting, the arrows aimed at Native people by other Native people, is a survival response rooted in a zero-sum equation where one tribe's share of federal resources can grow only at the expense of another tribe. (Let me digress for a moment: pitting tribes against one another, whether over federal funding, IBQ, or other Native identity issues, is a classic "divide and conquer" tactic.)

When I ran for election to serve on my tribe's Board of Directors, I learned that Native identity wasn't a matter of simple geography, a contradiction to what I'd experienced in college. After various jobs, I decided I wanted to work for my tribal community. It was important to me to raise my children among cousins and for them to attend the variety of cultural activities sponsored by our tribe. After more than a decade living and working in Sault Ste. Marie, I was local, no longer a newcomer. I met the residency requirement to run for elected office in the tribal district where I lived. I was confident in my chances . . . and was devastated when I didn't win. A few cousins who don't sugarcoat their opinions said I was from the side of the family that had "left the Rez when times were bad." See, my dad had left the area as a young man. He met and married my mother during his Navy years, and they raised us in a small town at the opposite end of the state. Although we frequently made the seven-hour drive back north for weddings, funerals, and powwows and spent time each summer visiting my grandparents and cousins, some family members would always see me as an outsider. They had created an even smaller, more exclusive circle within the Native identity bullseye of locals who lived within the reservation borders: the ones who stayed.

Losing hurt, and it was yet another experience that made me question my identity, one that I drew from in creating Daunis's character in *Firekeeper's Daughter*. In the story, her beloved Nish kwe role model Aunt Teddie makes a comment that reminds Daunis of her outsider status. Auntie later apologizes for the words that Daunis internalized as, *You're not really one of us*. When an "othering" remark comes from someone you admire, it is an arrow directly to the heart. I know my cousins weren't trying to be malicious when they told me why I hadn't won the election. I was a grown woman with children. And still, because I'd devoted my adult life to serving and uplifting Native people, because I'd spent the last decade working for my tribal community, I thought, *Maybe now they will see me as one of them, an equal, a true Nish kwe.*

It was around this time that I started to write *Firekeeper's Daughter.* I knew I wanted to tell the kind of story that I'd loved when I was young, ones with action and mystery and a strong, intelligent heroine. I also knew I needed to make identity a central part of the narrative. Daunis's Native identity is further complicated by the decision her maternal grandparents made to keep her Native father's name off her birth certificate. She yearns to be an enrolled citizen; however, she is unable to provide the required documentation connecting her to her (now-deceased) father.

Unlike Daunis, I've been an enrolled tribal citizen since childhood. My tribal card, issued from my tribe's enrollment office, includes my photo identification, an individual citizenship number, and a file number that identifies which branch of the tribal family tree I descend from. This card qualifies me to vote in tribal elections, sell artwork as an authentic Native American, possess eagle feathers, and get a discount on gasoline purchased at our tribal gas stations. If I apply for a job with my tribe or with certain federal agencies that serve

Native communities, my card provides documentation of my eligibility for Indian preference policies in hiring.

My laminated tribal ID card is not a shield. It offers little to no protection from the fluid bullseye of Native identity. There will always be someone telling me—or otherwise conveying—which circle they see me in.

About halfway through *Firekeeper's Daughter*, Daunis is able to apply for tribal citizenship when the Tribal Council passes a law that allows for other forms of documentation in lieu of a birth certificate. After a moment of joyous shock, she thinks to herself:

I have wanted this ever since I understood that being Anishinaabe and being an enrolled citizen weren't necessarily the same thing. [. . .] I can become a member. Except . . . it changes nothing about me.

I am Anishinaabe. Since my first breath. Even before, when my new spirit traveled here. I will be Anishinaabe even when my heart stops beating and I journey to the next world.

When I typed the declaration, I remember feeling a calm acceptance of its truth. My self-concept had, at last, caught up with what my spirit has always known. Native identity has a myriad of external definitions that I cannot control. Self-concept, however, is entirely internal. For much of my life, I looked outward in an effort to understand who I was. My self-concept is not bestowed by others—it is claimed and controlled solely by me. I am Anishinaabe—not fractions of an identity, but the whole that is greater than the sum of its parts.

Daunis's story is my story, except she defined her self-concept at age nineteen. I didn't claim my self-concept until I was in my mid-forties. Once I did, I felt an inner peace that was both comforting and exciting, both powerful and humbling. In writing her story and revealing parts of my own, I hope for readers to feel less alone and more connected.

I challenge you to rethink the Native identity bullseye. Instead of visualizing concentric circles intended to define and exclude, look at it from high above. To me, it resembles a bird's-eye view of our powwow grounds. At the center, the core of my spirit, is the drum that symbolizes a heartbeat—mine and that of Mother Earth. Each beat reverberates through the ground. When I dance around the drum, I feel it in the moccasins my dad made for me. At Grand Entry, the line of dancers circles the arena before wrapping around and continuing until everyone is present. The spiraling circles that flow from the center are filled with my family—those who came before me, those with me in this world, and those yet to arrive. And just like ripples in a pond, the connections emanate to reach others. I move through this life as the self I claim, and as part of something larger than my individual self. My self-concept is the shield that protects who I am at my core being.

Dearest reader, as you claim your self-concept, always remember that your worth is inherent and infinite.

Cheering you on,

Angeline

Excerpted passages from *Firekeeper's Daughter* by Angeline Boulley, published 2021 by Henry Holt Books for Young Readers

You never know what could be interesting tomorrow.

—Robbie Robertson (Cayuga, Mohawk)

PRIMITIVE

By Vera Starbard
(Tlingit, Dena'ina)

Primitive.

By nineteen, I already had a lifetime of holding back anger at all the slights and barbs and aggressions built up. And with one word, from one "well-meaning" workshop presenter, it found its inevitable release.

Primitive.

More than anger. In the last few years my carefully stuffed-down anger—the anger child therapists repeatedly told me to display despite not knowing its source—had grown to a pool of boiling fury.

You know, I think you're the first Native person I've had in any of my AP classes.

I think Alaska Natives are the ugliest race. Oh, but not you!

Isn't this apartment a bit south for a Native person? We don't usually have Natives apply.

And one day, in my college sociology class where we were discussing the recent scourge of rapes and murders targeting Alaska Native women in Anchorage, the professor posed the question, *Why is the public not outraged by this?*

The breathtakingly quick response from the all-white-except-me class was united: *We see Native women as less than human.*

The coldness with which they agreed on and discussed this was at first jarring. But as I sat there, trying to hold back tears, their cold and scientific certainty about my perceived animality helped me keep them at bay. *Keep that anger down. Don't let them make you an angry stereotype on top of this.*

Not that Tlingit women often defied that stereotype. Tlingit women of legend and Tlingit women of today are known among other Alaska Native groups as being ready to fight. Back in the day, the fights were literal life-and-death battles. Nowadays, the fights are with words, with laws, with activism—not life-and-death anymore. Or so I thought. And despite being a naturally "sensitive" kid (which translates in Tlingit as I was a big crybaby), I was raised to fight like a Tlingit woman. My mother may have sung my sister and me

Tlingit lullabies, but she also taught us to speak up when we saw injustice. My grandmother may make a killer nagoon berry jelly, but she also modeled how to insert yourself at the table to fight for your literal land. When I think of "sister," I think of mine physically inserting herself between myself and my abuser. When I think of "auntie," I think of innumerable women and ancestors stepping in to give me cookies and lessons in equal supply. My stories growing up were of Fog Woman demanding respect, of Elizabeth Peratrovich schooling white senators on the Bill of Rights. I may have been born with no fight and little strength, but until I had to stand on my own, I had a lifetime of Tlingit women lending me theirs.

And so, less than a year after that stunning realization of how others perceived me as a human, I maybe should have been prepared for how they saw our artwork. But I wasn't. I was listening to this white woman in an arts workshop describe Alaska Native art as she showed examples, including a totem pole carved by the Tlingit Master Artist I admired the most, Nathan Jackson.

The art may seem primitive, but I encourage you to check Alaska Native art out.

Primitive.

Primitive.

Primitive.

In the spectrum of racist actions and words I'd dealt with my whole life, up to and including physical threats, an off-hand remark about our art would, on the outside, seem pretty mild. And yet here it was. As I sat there in that room of white people, listening to this well-meaning white woman, that word "primitive" jumped out and proved to be the drop of water to unleash a childhood of holding back anger and spill the whole, swirling pool. The fury built up over the years and the inevitable release.

Except it wasn't fury that came out.

It was grief.

Unlike that day in sociology class, this time I let the tears fall. I couldn't stop them as I walked out of the building, and I didn't care who saw them. I just happened to pass by an older Tlingit woman, who had also spent her life around primarily white people on her own land. I didn't know her well, but when she saw me, she must have recognized something of a need in me. I told her the simple fact of what was said, and she sighed with a familiar weariness.

Oh, Vera. They just don't understand.

It didn't make me feel better, but it did make me feel less crazy.

You see, it had never occurred to me in my nineteen years of life that Tlingit art was anything but brilliant. Formline paint and woven Chilkat designs and carved cedar stories adorn everything we do. I was raised to fight, but I was also raised in a culture that highly valued both its art and its artists. We don't even have a word for "art." There's no separation between what the Western world calls "art" and the community's economy, or politics, or identity, or spirituality. Art is not a separate thing, and it is not a frivolous thing. And it certainly had never occurred to me that anyone could look at the complexity and skill involved in our visual art as anything but that. It never occurred to me we could be seen as primitive.

Now is when someone who has been paying attention to, oh, everything ever created about Native people in popular culture would ask, *Really? You really never saw Native people viewed as primitive?* I suppose feeling a little dumb was also in the grief. But it was still grief, nearly overwhelming grief as this word finally put that puzzle together for me. Suddenly, years of confusing comments finally made sense. I never understood the perspective of those flinging the barbs, and I suddenly did.

As a Native woman, maybe a majority of the people around me, on land my ancestors have held for over thirteen thousand years, see me as something closer to an animal. At best, an exotic interest; at worst, an infestation to be stamped out. As a Tlingit woman, I was also raised to constantly consider how everything I do and say and experience impacts my clan. My community. And so it was at a stoplight on the way home, I gasped with the full tonnage of grief hitting me. It was not the weight of my lifetime, but of decades of communal mistreatment. Of identities stolen and language taken and shame and shame and shame heaped on our heads for daring to live how we had always lived. Of entire generations lost. For what?

When I pass through that stoplight, I still have to take a careful breath.

In the days, and then weeks, and then years to follow, it felt like a habit to collect all these things stolen and lost and weakened and killed. All these people. I snatched knowledge from wherever I could, grieved its loss in our culture, added it to the ever-growing burden. One of the pillars of Tlingit culture is the communal grieving of loss and trauma. It takes years to process grief as a community, and it comes with ceremony and art and stories and song. And at the end, you come out of grief together. But that too was outlawed for a long time, right when we most needed to know how to grieve. I longed for a way of grieving like we used to know. Instead, we are left to grieve individually our greatest losses. When we come out of grief, we come out alone—or not at all. For a long time, I thought I'd never come out of my grief. I went over and over our loss, our overwhelming, inexhaustible loss, for well over a decade.

And then one day . . .

As much as my long period of grief began with a seemingly mild comment, so too did the moment I began to leave my grief behind. I was sitting with a group of playwrights, brought through strongly on the Western idea of staged storytelling, and nearly all of them were talking about the difficulty in working in a culture that didn't value what they did. The jokes over getting a "useful degree," not some arts degree. The snicker of a parent talking about their starving-artist child who would never get a real job. And I just couldn't join what was obviously a universal experience for them. I'd certainly been raised in the same American culture they had. But I had been nursed in an older culture that saw art as immensely important. It couldn't be separated from our very identity. And the thought occurred to me: Tlingit culture could really teach them something about how to treat artists. Just a thoughtful moment, and not something I was immediately cognizant of, but just a little bit of the heaviness of grief slipped away. Pride took its place.

Not too long later, I was watching interviews about domestic violence as research for a play I was writing. Again and again and again, I would hear the women comment about the treatment of women throughout history: "Women have always been treated like second-class citizens" and "Society has always accepted abuse toward its women." And I thought, *Not in my society.* Early American anthropological reports on Tlingit people remarked on the "curious equity of the sexes" in Tlingit culture. Everything is inherited through the mother, and your entire identity comes from her line. Your father's line is honored, but ultimately, it has no say in your upbringing. And that is no small thing. When power is not hoarded by one gender, when the female line is the most important factor in determining who you are, your treatment of genders is quite different. As is treatment of abuse. We knew this for millennia, practicing our "equity of the sexes." I pitied the Western cultures—the Western women—who never knew their power.

And a little more of that grief slipped away.

It was around this time that I really started to think about just how much the ills of the dominant society could be answered by the wisdom of the very cultures whose land they resided on. It was also around this time that I was able to not just *believe* our culture was much more than primitive but share it. I showcased and celebrated our Indigenous excellence with my art. That word we don't have a word for. As generations of Tlingit women knew before me, what I do is valuable, and needed, and integral to a working society.

Primitive.

It no longer stings, that word. I feel sorry for the people who can't see the beauty and complexity and answers right in front of them.

Primitive.

I still feel sorrow for the losses. I still feel anger. But I don't feel that sting anymore of those who think I am less than human. Who think I'm something that almost disappeared—or should have disappeared—when the great white sails first arrived on this land.

Our land. Our land, which, when they first arrived and we looked at them with no leadership of women, who couldn't survive on the land, who treated the ones we finally saw abhorrently, and we thought . . .

Primitive.

I BELONG

By charlie amáyá scott
(Diné)

I grew up in the heart of the Navajo Nation among red mesas and canyon walls with a love for reading. It was a love nurtured by my mother that I carried throughout my K–12 educational journey and that blossomed even more when I went to Brown University. I remember the first time that I was in the university library. I was surrounded by so many books and just kept casually picking one up after the other and paging through them. I was so enthralled that I completely lost track of time and was awkwardly kicked out because the library was closing. Still, though attending Brown was an experience that I am grateful for, it's also one that haunts me. Because it was at Brown that I became quite aware of what it truly means to be Native in America.

My love of reading was really a love of learning. I enjoyed each and every subject that was available to me. I remember being one of the few students who were offered calculus in high school, which was unheard of in my school district (and only possible because I had taken both honors geometry and algebra during my sophomore year). In addition to being academically bright, I was involved in student council, in the yearbook club, as the founder of my school's gay-straight alliance, and as a volunteer at various sporting events to raise money for my class's senior trip. School was where I shined the brightest, and I enjoyed every moment of it. So much so that I was accepted to Brown University, an Ivy League school that I did not know even existed until I applied.

I arrived at Brown, nervous and exhausted. I had only two large suitcases with me, one of them full of clothes and the other packed with dorm room essentials. I honestly had no idea what I had gotten myself into. My entire life, I had been told to do well in school, get good grades, and go to college—any college. I'd done those things, and I now found myself at one of the most prestigious universities in the US Empire in a new city where I knew nobody. And here I was, moving into my dorm room. I had only ever been to Brown once, and while the campus was just as green and beautiful as I remembered, it was very different from home. (Years later, I must admit that I still miss the campus . . . just a little.)

The first few months at Brown were the hardest time that I had ever experienced in my entire life at that point. I was surrounded by people who did not look like me and who said words that I had to Google. They seemed to understand everything that the professors were saying in class, whereas I struggled to follow. I remember one of my first assignments of the semester. It was a paper for an entry-level sociology course about symbolic interactionalism, and I felt great about it. I was certain that I'd get an A and prove to everyone, especially myself, that I belonged.

I got a C . . . minus.

Walking out of class that day, I cried. At that point, I'd been at Brown for a month and had done everything I could think of to excel. I stayed up until two almost every night studying—working and reworking math problems and reading and highlighting so many articles in an effort to understand theory. I took pages of notes while in class, only to realize that I could not comprehend them afterwards. Nothing seemed to be working, and the C minus was glaring evidence that maybe I did not belong here at all. I began to doubt myself, my intelligence and abilities, and my decision to attend Brown. I felt so alone, and no matter how hard I tried, no matter what I did, it felt like I was destined to fail.

I was distraught. I called my mom, and through my tears, I told her how much I hated it here and that I wanted to come home.

She listened until I told her everything and then said, "No. You are not coming home. You are going to stay there until the end of the semester, and then we will talk. You chose Brown— you chose to apply, and you chose to be there. You *do* belong. Do not let anyone else tell you otherwise, shiyazhí. It will get easier. . . ." She also pointed out that we didn't have the money to buy a last-minute plane ticket, a reality that I understood but something my wealthy classmates couldn't, which only made me feel like I *really* didn't belong. "Just get through this semester, shiyazhí," she reiterated, "and we'll talk about our options."

I agreed and ended the call, wiping the rest of my tears away while standing in the middle of the quad. For weeks, I had been holding on to the fear, the loneliness, and the anxiety. In that moment, hearing my mother's voice and crying were what I needed. My mom had reminded me of something that I'd forgotten—I chose Brown. I chose to be here. In this moment of clarity, I realized that even though I had been the best student in my high school, I was not the best student at Brown, and that was *okay*. I did not need to be the best student at Brown; I just needed to do *my* best. In retrospect, I have that C-minus paper to thank because I was able to release all of my bottled-up feelings and frustrations and really think about what to do next. Yes, getting a bad grade sucked, yet I would realize much later that this moment was connecting to something much bigger that I needed to unpack.

I also realized I could not do this alone. So, I scheduled meetings with professors and academic staff requesting extra guidance and support, including with the professor who had given me the C minus. In that meeting, I was humbled very quickly. He was honest about what was wrong with my paper and explained what he was looking for. I was starting to understand and asked what I could do better. He explained and also suggested that I go to the writing center. One of my other professors connected me with a tutor. All of this was new to me. I didn't know that you could ask for help and that it would be provided. I was so used to having to achieve on my own. The very thought of asking someone for help was absurd to me, but at Brown, it was necessary. If I was going to succeed, I needed support. Very quickly, the additional guidance shifted my college experience. My grasp of the material improved, and my studying was more effective, which resulted in better grades and boosted my confidence. My mom was right—things did get easier. One semester became two, then three, until finally, I graduated.

Almost a decade later, I still think about my first year at Brown, and the person who almost gave up on college because she felt like she did not belong in that kind of environment. I am grateful to the professors, the teaching assistants, the tutors, my advisors, administration, staff, and my friends, who offered support and kindness when I needed it. I wished that

I had been told that I could ask for help—it would have saved me from a lot of heartache and tears. I made myself invisible and tried to blend in. I tried to not be the only Native kid in the classroom. I wanted to be like my other classmates, but the reality was, I wasn't.

Now, someone reading this could assume that my public school education had not prepared me adequately for a university like Brown and that maybe I should have gone somewhere else. Another person reading this could argue that I was only accepted to Brown because I was Native and that I was lucky to get in and not fail. Who really knows? Not me. What I do know and have since learned is that the college educational system isn't set up for people like me to succeed, despite my love for reading and learning. Let me explain.

Imagine that there are one hundred Native students in a room. Can you guess how many would graduate from high school?

Seventy-five,* which is less than the 2019–2020 national average by 12 percent.

Now, of those seventy-five who graduated, can you guess how many would go on to college?

Twenty-one. That's roughly 28 percent, compared to the

---

*National Center for Education Statistics, "Public High School Graduation Rates," U.S. Department of Education, Institute of Education Sciences, 2023, accessed March 4, 2024, https://nces.ed.gov/programs/coe/indicator/coi.

2021 national average of 38 percent* of recent high school graduates enrolled in college.

Of those twenty-one, only nine will graduate within six years. (That's 42 percent; the national average is 64 percent.)** Essentially, fewer Native kids graduate from high school, and even fewer enroll and graduate from college. This is the state of education for Native students in America.

I share these dismal numbers not to glorify the few who get their degrees, but rather to highlight how isolating college can be for Native students and how that feeling of isolation can impact the college experience. As a first-year in college, I had assumed that my struggles were related to my academic failings. Many students, Native and non-Native, have a hard time their first year at college; I just thought I was one of them. But for Native students, our challenges run deeper. We struggle with feeling like we belong in places that were built on our removal, our displacement, and our genocide.

When I went to Brown, I knew nothing about the history of colonization that occurred for a place like Brown to exist. I

---

*Postsecondary National Policy Institute, "Native American Students in Higher Education Factsheet," updated November 22, 2023, https://pnpi.org/download /native-american-students-in-higher-education-factsheet/.

**Postsecondary National Policy Institute, "Native American Students in Higher Education Factsheet," updated November 22, 2023, https://pnpi.org/download /native-american-students-in-higher-education-factsheet/.

did not know what it meant to be Native in America because I grew up with my language and culture in a space that celebrated all of me. But that didn't happen at a place like Brown. I woke up to buildings instead of the mesas, to sirens instead of birds chirping. I never heard my language spoken. Nothing familiar existed. I felt like an anomaly and an outsider because nothing about me or my culture was celebrated at Brown. I tried to fit in and failed. And I felt bad for not fitting in. But I grew up in the Navajo Nation—what did I know about fitting in with non-Native kids? Maybe my first year at Brown would have been different if there were more from my community with me at Brown (fewer than 0.5 percent of the enrolled student population identifies as Native).[*] Maybe if home had been closer, Brown would have been different.

Since graduating, I've learned a lot more about the state of Native education in the US Empire, which has helped me process my own college experience. In a 1991 article, Kirkness and Barnhardt[**] emphasize the need for colleges and universities to respect, offer reciprocity, be relevant, and acknowledge the responsibilities of Native students. In *Beyond*

---

[*]"Brown University," Data USA, 2021, accessed March 4, 2024, https://datausa.io/profile/university/brown-university#enrollment_race.

[**]Kirkness, Verna J. and Ray Barnhardt, "First Nations and Higher Education: The Four R's—Respect, Relevance, Reciprocity, Responsibility," *The Journal of American Indian Education* 30 (1991): 1-15, https://www.jstor.org/stable/24397980.

Access: Indigenizing Programs for Native American Student Success (Routledge, 2018), the book's editors celebrate the access programs and structures that exist to support Native students while also highlighting some that did not do so well. I've read articles by Bryan McKinley Jones Brayboy, a Lumbee scholar, who discusses experiences of in/visibility and cultural integrity, and *Native Presence and Sovereignty in College: Sustaining Indigenous Weapons to Defeat Systemic Monsters* (Teachers College Press, 2022), a book by Amanda Tachine, a Diné scholar, which details how to showcase and celebrate cultural knowledge in order to navigate and survive college. After doing all of this research, I realized that the problem wasn't me, it was the systems and environments that have allowed Native students to struggle and that reinforce our struggle.

I know this now, especially as a doctoral candidate in higher education. This research has inspired the topic of my doctoral dissertation and reminds me of how important it is for students, especially Native students, for us, to be reminded of our brilliance and celebrated. I am well aware of how difficult college can be and still is for us, and I want to share a few reminders with you.

First, always remember that you carry generations of knowledge and herstories that are unique to us and our communities. I made the mistake of trying to fit in at a place like Brown and

I diminished who I was, where I come from, everything that I loved about myself, my culture, and my community.

Second, ask questions. Anyone and everyone, whether it is your residential advisor, the teaching assistants, professors, other students, they are there to learn and support you however they can. Ask questions and be curious. College is about exploration and learning, so be a little bit brave and ask questions.

Third, find community. My first week at Brown, I met my best friend, and, together, we survived Brown. She's from Georgia and is a Black woman who will become a doctor (very soon). We never would have met if I didn't accept an invitation to go shopping with another friend. Be willing to take chances and build community with others outside your own. She's taught me so much about what it means to be Black in America and I have shared with her about what it means to be Native in America.

I want to leave you with one more thought: You belong. Every day, Indigenous Peoples are made to feel like we do not belong, especially on stolen land. That is a lie. You belong; I belong; we all belong. You made a choice to be in that classroom, in that school, in that studio, in any space that has refused people like us—always remember that you decided to be there. You *deserve* to be there. I am so proud of you and what you will accomplish. Have a beautiful day and remember, take care of yourself, okay?

INDIGENOUS QUEEN: FINDING THE RAINBOW WITHIN

By Lady Shug
(Diné)

When we come into the Earth, the first colors we see are gray. But when I arrived, my eyes saw all the colors of the rainbow.

I was especially attracted to the color pink and anything shiny and sparkly. As a child, I ran around with a towel on my head, an expression of my desire for long, flowing hair. I played with dolls, then trucks, then dolls again. I had a feminine power that sparkled and an inner fire that glowed. But that sparkle was discouraged. My family's idea of gender roles was steeped in religion and colonization. Pink was for girls, and when they looked at me, all they could see was blue. My spark was muted, my fire contained.

Growing up on a ranch on my Diné reservation in Crownpoint, New Mexico, I was isolated. The border of our territory was two hours away, and I spent much of my youth alone. In truth, my only friends were animals. School was a source of terrible anxiety. I went to an all-Indigenous school, and even though I looked like my classmates, I knew that I was different . . . and so did they. Although I kept my fire power bottled up and my colors muted, I was teased and ridiculed for being too feminine, too queer. Bullied daily, I couldn't use the school bathroom, and my peers often tried to fight me. I cried myself to sleep many nights.

I was desperate to meet other people like me, but coming across an out queer or trans person was very unusual. A lot of times I had deep, dark energy and bad thoughts of giving up, but I found hope in the music, art, and agriculture surrounding me. And from that hope, I built a character of survival, a persona that kept me safe from getting teased and bullied. This character was created to make my peers and family feel comfortable being around a queer person . . . and left me feeling uncomfortable in my own skin. But simmering beneath the surface was a power I didn't know that I had, one that I finally released at the end of senior year, when I knew I would be moving away from the reservation for college. Leaving my family, my land, and my home was very hard—but it was that journey of self-discovery that set me walking on the path toward the fabulous art of drag.

College felt like a total restart—after so many years of burying my feelings and power, I could be a more authentic version of myself. I threw myself into art classes and cheerleading and other interests. And in college, I met other queer and trans people for the first time. They made me feel seen in a way I never had before. It was with them that I saw my first drag show. Drag was something I had only ever seen in movies. But standing in Hamburger Mary's in Las Vegas watching ChiChi Dela Cruz changed my life. Drag was something I never knew that I needed or wanted to do. But the first time I painted my face, put on a gown, and donned a glamorous wig, I just *knew* that this was something I was meant to do and be. It was like a lightbulb had gone off! Yes, it was one of the scariest moments of my life—looking in the mirror, I had the sensation that I was about to be thrown from an airplane—but it was also thrilling. Not long after, I was compelled to take the stage by my drag mentor, CoCo Vega. As I stepped into the spotlight, all the pain and bullying and negativity I'd experienced seemed to dissipate. The inner power and strength that I'd been suppressing exploded! I felt comfortable! I felt beautiful! I felt *seen*. I was finally able to live fully in my feminine strength, assuming a great power that I never knew I had.

Despite the joy I found in this new outlet, the trauma of my younger life continued to fill me with self-doubt and feelings of unworthiness. By this point, I had finished college and was living in Las Vegas. Though I was grateful to be surrounded by passionate queens and talented performers, I deeply felt the lack of scenery in my surroundings and missed waking up to the clear skies and beauty of my own land. I didn't see how I could reconcile my true self with my true home, and these feelings grew very heavy. I fell into a depression and attempted suicide.

One day, despite having launched a successful career in the "Entertainment Capital of the World," I was called back to my territory—my homeland—and I took it. Going back to no running water or electricity after having all the amenities of a modern city was a difficult test of its own—but this time, I had the power of drag in my back pocket. I returned with the strength and power I never knew I had when I was little. I carried the embers of my own fire back home to my people and my land. Today, I'm still creating space for queer and trans relatives on and off our Indigenous territories.

Near the end of every season of *RuPaul's Drag Race*, RuPaul asks the remaining queens what they would tell their younger selves. It's something I've thought a lot about. I would say: *You are going to do a lot mentally and physically. It's not going to be simple. When you find yourself in a dark space, rely on the land. Rely on our four-legged relatives. Rely on the family whom you trust, even if they don't completely understand. Give yourself to the land—it's a living being.*

I now live authentically in my queer, feminine power. On and off my territories, I'm proud of who I am and where I come from. Sometimes people tell me that I'm not Indigenous enough and that I shouldn't be the voice of queer Indigenous folks. It used to bother me, but no longer. I've never tried to tell anyone how to be, and I'm not speaking for anyone but myself. I live by the mantra that our existence is our own form of resistance. Nobody can tell you who to be or take away who you are.

My story is one of millions. The Creator designed different pathways so we can find ourselves and walk our true path. We are all relatives. Love your culture, love the land, and love yourself.

THE AG WORKERS' DAUGHTER

By Cece Meadows

(Xicana, Yoeme)

Fresh strawberries, crispy lettuce, humongous artichokes, tasty broccolini, picked and boxed by the hands of our mothers, fathers, grandparents, tías and tíos. Working in the hot scorching sun, picking your food for pennies on the dollar, trying to hit that daily quota or they won't get paid. Eating and rehydrating, resting for just a moment will cost them the day.

Xicanos, Indigenous people, called cheap laborers and ilegales, working the lands of our ancestors on farms that once belonged to us. Don't they get tired of making up names for

us? We are the never-respected peoples who work hard to provide for their familias, only innocents whom they rob and
mistreat. Disposable bodies who endure the deadly heat and
violent rays. Stolen braceros who return to our homelands in
Mexico, empty-handed, robbed, and owed millions.

Raising and protecting my youngest siblings, trying to shield
them from the bullets flying through our windows. Mis papás
missing special occasions, school events, championships, and
awards assemblies, la corrida keeps them enslaved for dreams
of our better opportunities. It never made me mad, just sad
they never got to see me accept awards and achieve accolades
I dedicated to them each and every time.

The "golden child," they call me, the one who makes it out.
The interpreter, the educated one, the loudmouth screaming for justicia, fairness, and land back! I've worn the fancy
black business suits, sat in their corporate boardrooms, learning their lingo and the truth to how they built generational
wealth—and this country—on the backs of my ancestors.

*   *   *

So, I walk in my destiny, on the prayers and orgullo de mi familia, soaking up knowledge, creating connections with allies, and bonding with like-minded friends who become relatives. Hustlers, hard workers, never waiting for things to be handed to us. Rooted in cultura, música, danza, y ceremonia. Somos semillas, the ample harvest, a blessing of a new sunrise, the most beautiful flowers that bloom.

I am proudly the ag workers' daughter.

THE DISCOVERY OF IRONY

By Philip J. Deloria
(Ihanktonwan Dakota Descendant)

My father was one of the world's more famous Indians. I'm not saying he was the *most* famous Indian, but he was right up there. In 1969, when I was ten years old, he had published a book, *Custer Died for Your Sins: An Indian Manifesto*, which became a bestseller. In the years that followed, the books and articles poured out of his typewriter: *We Talk, You Listen*; *Red Man in the New World Drama Revisited*; *Indians of the Pacific Northwest*; *God Is Red*; *The Indian Affair*; *Of Utmost Good Faith*; *Behind the Trail of Broken Treaties*; and more. The books beget lectures, and the lectures beget congressional testimony, boards, and consultations, and those things beget travel, which meant that he was on the road much of the time. It was a curious way to grow up. If my father was often missing in parental action, it was because he was part of a larger project of Native survivance, of which the family was all aware. Though we started out in genteel poverty, we ascended—to our great surprise—into a Native intellectual middle class, funded by those books and visible when my dad traded in the old green Ford for a red Oldsmobile. My brother, sister, and I came of age in a mixed-race suburban nuclear family, not a Native community, but we were inevitably tuned in to the realities of Indian politics.

In 1970, my father decided to move the family from Colorado to Bellingham, Washington, for a teaching job at what was then called Western Washington State College. We traded sunny skies for the Northwest coastal damp, and I'd be lying if I said it was easy. Everything about that time was hard, confused, and confusing—and not only for me. The Sixties weren't quite over, culturally, but the Seventies had formally arrived. Martin Luther King and Bobby Kennedy were dead, the Summer of Love was a distant memory, and the counterculture and Civil Rights movements seemed tired out, struggling to respond to a darker world. I was aware of these disappointments—emotionally, for sure; intellectually, maybe—and took them as the context for my new life in the rain.

For Indian folks, there's an idea frequently expressed of which I'm no fan. It's called "living in two worlds": there's an Indian world and a white world, and you toggle between the binary, always unsure of your footing. Bellingham (like life) proved much more complicated, and I felt torn up and uncertain in about ten different ways (not just two). My father was the token Indian in a newly formed ethnic studies department, so we made friends with the Black faculty member and the Chicano one too. My brother and I hung out with the countercultural white guy and his family, and we spent weekends at a certified hippie commune. At the commune, we ate cereal serially from a single bowl, saving the extra milk for the next user. We perambulated the city dump on salvage missions. We helped the guy building an octagonal house with a circular saw, his strung-together electrical cords snaking over to the next lot. There was a tipi, occupied by soapstone carvers, that got soggy in the rain. Once we tried to roast a pig in a pit, though everyone got hungry and pulled it out long before it had cooked. It was woodsy living, with high spirits and cheerful incompetence.

Then there were the lessons in class politics. We moved into a curiously mod farmhouse, with a big barn, an old Christmas-tree lot, a massive sawdust pile created by a long-vanished mill, rooms full of mechanical farm junk waiting to be salvaged, cherry trees and blackberry bushes, and a concrete fishpond full of massive goldfish. There were two small houses across the road, the former homes of farmworkers and now occupied by a working-class white family and a mixed Native family.

My parents believed that there were lessons to be learned through labor. The day after we moved in, I found myself wedged between the neighbor boys, on a school bus heading to the fields where we would pick strawberries, raspberries, and beans. Mostly strawberries. A flat—twelve quart-sized boxes—would earn seven cents. I worked a full summer and brought home something like forty-two dollars. I watched migrant workers pick five times as much as me, even as I felt in my bones the challenge of the fieldworker: Kneel for a while until your knees ache; then stoop for a while until your back cries out. Do not take breaks. Breathe the pesticides.

As a kid in Bellingham, then, I picked up a bit of the emergent multicultural world of academic ethnic studies. I was seduced by the weirdness of a big house full of odd and interesting people, each doing their thing in the hippiest way possible. And I came to know stoop labor and—though I felt it more than understood it—the realities of proletarianization and the oppressions of capital. For wasn't the big-time farmer who hired the school bus and the child workers and the migrants more or less the same guy who had built the house with the fishpond and the workers' quarters in which my friends lived?

These were years when my grandparents seemed to visit with some frequency. My grandfather showed up in Bellingham from South Dakota, wanting to teach us a few things. He was a fabulous athlete, so throwing, catching, running, and tackling were always first on the agenda. But there was also storytelling, and lots of it. Our family was from Yankton, but he'd grown up at Standing Rock and then worked at Pine Ridge, Rosebud, and Sisseton. He had been collecting songs and stories from across 'akota country for his entire life. When he arrived at our house, it was time to pull out the reel-to-reel. He loved to be recorded and left behind a trail of tapes wherever he went. To this day I still receive the occasional worn box containing a reel of crinkled audiotape rediscovered in someone's attic. What he was also doing, of course, was teaching us a corpus of cultural narrative: the woman saved by the wolves, the vision of Red Leaf, the Iktomi cycle, the story of the White Buffalo Calf Woman and the sacred pipe, a ghost story or five, and many more. He took pleasure in the sound of the Lakota language and the power of song, and if we did not have enough time or intensity to learn what he knew, at least he'd tried to give us an introductory education.

These were also the years when I took a first pass at reading my father's books. I started with *Custer Died for Your Sins*—and to be precise, the chapter titled "Indian Humor." Those who have read *Custer* will understand that the first half offers biting criticism: of the federal government, of anthropologists, of churches and missionaries. The second half turns to future possibilities, asking what it would look like for America to embrace what my dad called "tribalism." The humor chapter bridges these two sections. It is something like an Indian stand-up routine, a fast-paced romp through all the jokes he and his pals were telling at the meetings of the National Congress of American Indians. They've lost some of their salience today: Who remembers that a company called "Arrow" once made and advertised men's dress shirts, such that the line "Custer wore an Arrow shirt" was once funny? The chapter was legible to an eleven-year-old, however, and it paired well with my grandfather's story sessions. Warmed up by Indian humor, I tackled the rest of the book, and it made up a second, critical part of my cultural education.

And these were the years when the Lummi Nation was building what would become its successful aquaculture business. Our odd little farmstead was only a mile or so from tribal headquarters, and my dad was close friends with Wally Heath, a marine biologist who proposed the original aquaculture effort. In 1969, the Lummi people had built a small pond for oyster, trout, and salmon. In 1971, they raced against time and tide to complete a much larger one. A parade of trucks raced in and out along the dike, dumping fill material, and we kept an anxious eye out, praying that they would make it. They did. My father's writing turned to the Northwest, and he grew close to the Lummi leadership. We celebrated at the annual Stommish festival, relishing the open-fire smoked salmon. Some nights a few fishers would appear at the door with a hoop of oysters. We'd all sit on the floor, cracking shells and slurping the oysters down. Those were good moments and good folks, and not forgotten. When my dad passed, we donated his library to Northwest Indian College; the college has hosted an annual Vine Deloria Jr. Indigenous Studies Symposium for nearly two decades.

It is not easy to move to a new town when one is eleven years old, and I ended up at the bottom of the social world of Shuksan Middle School. I dressed a little funny, I'll admit, and I wore shoes—meant to correct my fallen arches—that looked something like a businessman's wing tips. I was a nerdy band kid who carried a bulky trombone on the bus each day (because I actually practiced most nights). I was that kind of kid. And where my brother and sister looked a lot like my dad, I took after my mother's Swedish-Swiss ancestry. That mattered to the story I want to tell.

The school bus started the day picking up Lummi kids from the reservation, and they would cluster at the back of the bus, seizing the prime territory, talking loudly and lapsing occasionally into disorder. A funny thing happened, though, as the bus took its path into town. The kids at the stops got whiter and older as the route moved through Bellingham's suburbs (for efficiency's sake, the bus mixed middle schoolers and high schoolers together). As those kids boarded, the Indian kids lost their groove, growing silent as the social world of the bus transformed along racial lines. Suddenly, one realized that the place was segregated and that the back rows in Bellingham were not unlike those in Montgomery in the days before Rosa Parks and the bus boycotts. It was just that it was Indian kids rather than Black workers who occupied the back.

But now imagine the reverse trip, from the school back to the Lummi Reservation. With every stop, the bus lost a few white high schoolers, and the percentage of Native kids went up. The Lummis reemerged as a force to be reckoned with, and what was both cool and frightening was the way their school bus noise was often flat-out political. Their parents had fought against a magnesium-oxide reduction plant that would have destroyed Lummi Bay—indeed that fight had led to the aquaculture project. Everyone had been watching the fishing rights struggles playing out at places like Frank's Landing on the Nisqually and Cooks Landing on the Columbia, where fish-and-game cops beat up and abused Indians. And who among them wasn't aware of the works of Native activists and lawyers like my father, each arguing for a new place for Indians and a movement called Red Power?

The bus was not simply the usual cauldron of adolescent school stuff. It was a complicated stew of adolescent school stuff, anti-racist anger, anti-colonial critique, and plain badass toughness, infused with local history and the national anxieties that clung to the years surrounding 1970. When things got tense on the bus, was there a better target than the new kid, on the pale side, sitting by himself with goofy shoes and a trombone?

So it was that one day, an older Lummi kid named Jimmy lost it on me. He smacked my face against the window and pushed so hard I thought the glass might break, yelling at me about the stolen land whizzing by outside. It was probably a pretty good accounting of the wrongs done along the Nooksack River and Bellingham Bay, and he closed it off with a radical slogan: "Custer died for your sins, man; Custer died for your *sins!*"

It was ridiculous and funny, and what was I to say? Because, in a general way, he wasn't wrong. If you take a family tree back far enough you find all kinds: my mom's grandparents' generation who had tried (and failed) to homestead in northeast Colorado; my dad's great-grandfather Alfred Sully, who had led ethnic cleansing on the northern plains in the 1860s; my paternal grandmother's eighteenth-century ancestors, who negotiated their own Indian land deed for the town that would become Sloatsburg, New York. On the other side of the ledger, though, there was my dad, my uncle, my great-aunts, my great-grandfather, and my great-great, the Yankton band leader Saswe. My own grandfather was making sure I knew about those people too.

So what was I to say to Jimmy? *Ummm . . . hey! My dad made up your political slogan!*? I just stayed silent and took the medicine.

Because that's what it was. Though I couldn't articulate it, and he didn't know it, Jimmy taught me something important: that being Indian puts you in an inescapable condition of irony. Iron-y. *Máza-ska.* There is the way things *are* and there is the way things are *described*, and Native folks cannot unsee the distinction. United States describes itself as a land of liberty? For some settlers, maybe, but not Native peoples. America celebrates immigration and the frontier? What about conquest and death? Americans describe Indians as vanished and gone. But that's not true, is it? When colonized people listen to the words of their colonizers, they can't help but hear irony.

And irony, it turns out, is the root of much humor and, as Gerald Vizenor would later suggest, it's a key component in Native survivance. Irony sharpens up your critical faculties. Indian people have prospered—despite the circumstances— by turning pain into humor, which *also* relies upon the gap between what it *is* and what people say it is. Custer dies full of arrows (true); Custer dies in an Arrow shirt (not true but borrowed from a description of reality). Jimmy borrows "Custer died for your sins" from my father while smashing my face, and the situation mingles pain and a hilarious absurdity. Humor acknowledges the structure but makes the teller a protagonist, a person of agency.

And thus, I came to realize dimly, as an eleven-year-old, not-quite-ready, wannabe reader of *Custer Died for Your Sins*, that to make sense of its wit and sarcasm, you had to appreciate the jokes in the chapter on Indian humor. Those jokes rest on the pain of irony, which rests on the hurts of history, which are inescapable, but which do not control or define us.

This is for every little Rez kid, every little urban kid, every little Native kid out there who has a dream, who is seeing themselves represented and our stories told by ourselves, in our own words.

—Lily Gladstone (Siksikaitsitapi, Nimiipuu)

THE BIRTH OF AN INDIGENOUS FOOD WARRIOR

By Crystal Wahpepah
(Kickapoo)

No matter the time of the year, it's always chilly on San Francisco Bay. But on this morning—November 23, 2023—at Pier 33, I am warm, filled from within by a fire to feed my community. For the first time, the elders, tribal leaders, and dancers returning from the annual Gathering on Alcatraz will be eating Indigenous food made by an Indigenous food warrior. The Kickapoo burritos my staff and I are making will be filled with the three sisters—squash, beans, and corn—that remain sacred to the representatives of the more than three hundred tribes and nearly six thousand people who rise early every year to honor the Ohlone people, the first inhabitants of this land, on a day the majority of our country feast on a myth and football.

I am not bitter or mourning in any way. I am celebrating because this is a real full-circle moment for me. My aunts and my mother had been part of the Indians of All Tribes movement that occupied Alcatraz between 1969 and 1971. My late uncle, Bill Wahpepah, was one of the founders of the Indigenous Peoples Gathering Sunrise Ceremony back in 1975 when he served as a leader within the International Indian Treaty Council. Morning Star Gali, whom I have known all my life, is one of the organizers of this year's event. And here I am, serving my people their food.

I remember those frigid journeys across the bay as a child—the clothes, the colors, the passion in the voices calling for recognition, dignity, and basic human rights. My extended family and their friends talked about Indian housing, Indian health care, erasure, education, everything. The meals at La Peña afterwards were where the first tender shoots of becoming a Native chef sprouted. At around the age of seven, I began asking the questions: *Where are our foods? Why are our foods never on menus or served in restaurants?* How was it that a city like Oakland, which was home to tens of thousands of Native Americans, had no place that served my grandmother's corn soup?

Even at that young age, I already understood there was a big difference between the food that came in a box and the colorful, delicious food of the ancestors. Those boxes contained the foods of convenience and industry, meant to make things cheap and easy, but they did not honor Creation, which calls on us to pay attention to our food, how it is grown, and how it is prepared. It was just another tactic to separate us from ourselves, just like the boarding schools that stripped my grandparents and my mother of their names, their language, and their faith, all to eradicate the "Indian" inside of them. My uncle Bill, however, taught me to be proud of who I am and all the different parts that made me.

Native foods are where I found myself and my home. Throughout my childhood, my sister and I often lived with other family members. My grandfather would take me berry picking when I was barely big enough to carry a basket. I thought of the sweet, plump deep purple blackberries as my friends, and when things were rough at home, I would escape to untamed brambles and fields around the Kickapoo Reservation in McLoud, Oklahoma, and find my center among the berries. By the time I was eleven, I had lived with aunts and uncles throughout the United States and Canada. While on the Hoopa Valley reservation with my aunts Jennie Cardova and Carleta Billy, I found peace in picking huckleberries, blueberries, elderberries, and pine nuts, whatever was in season. Aunt Jennie would make pies for me, and I took comfort in that cycle of foraging from the land and tasting its sweetness. During my time in Canada, wild strawberries plucked from low bushes filled my belly with such goodness.

The more I learned and the more I reconnected with the soil, the seeds, and the stories, the more I found my voice in the food sovereignty movement. The more I traveled on this mission, the more I connected with activists such as Linda Black Elk, who has become my sister in traditional ecological knowledge and the healing properties of whole, natural foods. It is traumatizing for people who are connected to the land to see the land being abused. It is like seeing a member of your family beaten, bruised, broken. By becoming reconnected to these foods that come from our Earth, we are not only healing our broken bodies but transforming the generational trauma into strength. By sharing our foods with the community, we are helping our neighbors heal.

After high school, I attended the American Indian College in Phoenix to study business. All along, I worked in restaurants, in both back-of-house and front-of-house positions, to make ends meet, even after I gave birth to three daughters. From 2008 to 2010, I attended culinary school in San Francisco. I didn't graduate—trying to balance being a full-time student and a working mother proved too much. Still, I left school with some valuable new skills that helped me on my journey of bringing Native American cuisine to restaurant tables so that we could celebrate a rich and long heritage of honoring the land and waters and what they provided beyond sustenance. I took a leap and launched a catering business called Wahpepah's Kitchen. My first client was the Native American Health Center in Oakland, but I soon caught the attention of businesses in Silicon Valley. I used every event to talk about Indigenous foodways, using as many ingredients by Native growers and producers as I could find. I grew close with the people at the Cultural Conservancy, a Native-led Bay Area nonprofit that, among many things, grows food from heirloom seeds gathered from Native communities.

Bonney Hartley, a member of the Stockbridge-Munsee Mohican Nation, was the director of community services at Native American Health, and she heard about a business incubation program called La Cocina. In 2010, she and wellness counselor Katherine Lewis offered to sponsor me for the program so I could connect with mentors and develop Wahpepah's Kitchen even further. So, when a restaurant space became available at the Fruitvale Station in Oakland, I was prepared to open the doors to my own place. It would be a place that served not only my grandmother's corn soup but also deer sticks with a chokecherry dipping sauce, Kickapoo chili, and pine tea.

Wahpepah's Kitchen is my way of helping my community heal. The first day the restaurant was open, an older man came in and ordered the blue corn cake. As he ate it, he began to cry. He had not been home to his reservation since he was eighteen years old, he said, and eating these foods was like leading him home. When he thanked me, I knew—in spite of all my fear of taking on the responsibility of a brick-and-mortar space—that I was on the right road.

THE SERPENT'S MOUTH

By Madison Hammond
(San Felipe Pueblo, Navajo, Black)

When I was a kid, going to the beach was a special rarity. The water and coastline were a stark contrast to the brown landscape I saw from the tiny Pueblo of San Felipe in my home of New Mexico. I grew up far from any beaches, but soccer tournaments gave me a glimpse of them, and a cross-country move when I was eight brought me close to one in Virginia. But still, we never went to the beach for extended days. These were pit stops or, at best, day trips, not the weeklong vacations that I imagined rich people took. To me, the beach was a gift. I remember the smell as the highway became a straightaway to the water, the air changing slightly and filling me with an anticipation and joy that was hardly containable. The skies seemed to open up in a different way as the trees became scarce. Closer to the ocean, sunscreen stained the air, and sand whipped between the rows of parked cars.

One of those miscellaneous trips has become a moment ingrained in my memory. I was nine years old, and we took a trip to Ocean City. I spent hours making sand fortresses and then watched as the sea cut through them. The rhythm of the waves created a reliable beat and mesmerized me. I remember my mom and sister walking out to enjoy the water and my grandma relaxing in a chair behind us. My sister and I bodysurfed in the icy Mid-Atlantic water and then let the sun rays dry us.

At some point in the day, there was a brief lag in the waves, a moment when the crashing became small like vibrations instead of beating drums. My grandma got out of her chair and joined me close at the water's edge. She took my hand, and we started drawing in the sand with our toes, where the bubbles from the waves fizzled and disappeared into the sand.

"Did you know that the ocean is the opening of the serpent's mouth?" she asked.

I glanced up at her in confusion.

"The water serpent is our greatest protector, and the serpent's mouth is here where the end of the earth meets the water," she explained. "The beach is the most sacred place in the world because it's the source of our powers and inner strength. It is what gives us blessings like precious rainfall in the summers."

I looked out to the sea, which now seemed limitless. My grandma took cornmeal from a beaded pouch that she carried around with her and placed a pinch's worth in the salty palm of my hand, an offering to the Creator.

"Now, look out to the ocean, Shrewka"—my given Indian name, which means "Magpie"—"then close your eyes and say a prayer to the Creator."

I did as she told, squeezing my eyes tight and saying my prayers to myself. I let the cornmeal fly into the water, watching my wishes become a part of the waves as they continued beating in rhythm against the earth.

Now, at twenty-six years old, I live far from my Pueblo of San Felipe, but the water serpent has followed me everywhere I go. It is on the pottery and some decor in my apartment in Los Angeles. My journey as a professional footballer has taken me to many different places, but the coastline has again become my home. The beach, which was once a day trip, a down-and-back, a fleeting moment of clarity and peace, is a place that is now so accessible and close to me.

The strength that I find from the water, from the serpent's mouth, extends to me onto the soccer field. And that strength is close to me now, at the beach, but also at a small Pueblo just north of Albuquerque, New Mexico, within a community that I can rely on wherever I am in the world. I had always wished to become a professional footballer, though it took me some time to realize and find the amount of courage, patience, and belief that I would need to accomplish the dream. When I "became" the first Native American to play in the National Women's Soccer League, I quickly learned that believing in myself wasn't enough. I needed to rely on others, so I drew from the belief that I have in my people, our ceremonial traditions, and the intangible power we draw from our surroundings. The strength I get from them is just as important as the daily work I do to play football at the highest level. And now I get to play in front of twenty thousand fans almost every weekend. Most days, I don't feel total clarity and peace, and there are days where I am searching for the next big moment or for another wish. It's on those days that I can go to the beach, thank the Creator, the serpent, my community, and also myself for where I have arrived.

I don't remember what I prayed for on the beach with my grandma that day. But sometimes I think that maybe it was to end up exactly where I am today.

DEAR REZ KID

By Ahsaki LaFrance-Chachere
(Diné, African American)

Dear Rez Kid,

My name is Ahsaki LaFrance-Chachere. I am from the Wateredge People, born for the African American People. My maternal grandfather's clan is the Cliff-Dwelling People, and my paternal grandfather's clan is the African American People. My four clans, my two sets of ancestors, my origins, and my homeland of Besh-be-toh (Iron Water), Arizona, have defined me as a proud, unapologetic Diné (Navajo)–Black woman. I am a daughter, granddaughter, wife, sister, aunt, and business-woman. If you'll allow me, I'd like to share some advice that I have found useful in my journey.

When you wake up in the morning, look at the horizon as Grandfather sun greets you. Whether you are on your reservation or not, I still want you to admire the beautiful Rez-blue sky. Remember, no matter where you are, this is our ancestors' land. You are always home. I say this as someone who travels a lot. I have found that this mind-set has made me stronger, particularly in the big city, which can swallow you. But if you remind yourself that you are always at home, that you are never alone, you will look at the world a little differently.

Dream big, dear reader, and never doubt yourself about going after your goals. I know firsthand what it is like to be a "Rez kid." I too grew up without running water and electricity. I attended the reservation public school before going to college. I worked for my tribal government. I know how it is to navigate life with almost no resources on the reservation. Still, I did not let anything stop me from chasing my dreams. From a young age, I knew that I wanted to build businesses that would have a major impact on and off the reservation, ones that would create and bring resources to my reservation, across Native Nations, and throughout the world. As my dreams took shape, they got bigger and bigger. I wanted my businesses to compete with the top businesses around the world—do not underestimate Native Empires! I did not let the overregulated and oppressive system stop me from doing what everyone told me was impossible. Breaking into the beauty industry was daunting—how could a Rez Brand compete with the leading companies?—but I took this as a challenge and set out to prove that a Rez Brand could be successful too. Many of my dreams have come true; I continue to chase others. It is okay to dream those big dreams that seem impossible for a Rez kid. You can truly do everything your heart desires.

I am a testimony to that. I created the first Native American prestige beauty brand in the country. Ah-Shi Beauty is not just an ordinary beauty brand—it Indigenized the beauty industry.

When I was little, I loved watching my mom get ready, watching her pick her outfits, adorn herself in turquoise, and apply her beauty routine. She'd start by mixing a few foundations together to create the right shade to match her skin tone. (It was something all the women in my family did.) It always bothered me, watching my mom being forced to be her own color chemist. We'd go to the malls in Phoenix, Arizona, a five-hour drive from our reservation, to shop at my mom's favorite designer stores, which were adorned with images of beautiful models, none of whom looked like us, so that my mom could then drive all the way home and concoct her own foundation? I knew at an early age that this was a problem. Little did I know that this would be the root of why I built Ah-Shi Beauty.

As I got older, I became more aware of the differences between reservation life and the off-the-reservation lifestyle. I am very proud of our Rez Life, and I picked up on the fact that in the somewhat pretentious beauty world, Rez Life didn't seem to have a place. High-end beauty brands showcase a lifestyle that feels far from the reservation and makes it seem like our Rez Life can't be luxurious. But I saw beauty and luxury all around me, in our land, culture, and language. In the faces of our ancestors. In the jewelry and textiles that grace our bodies. A vision of what my business could be started to form. Certainly, it would offer our people foundations that would match their skin tone! But way more than that, I wanted to create a brand that anyone on the reservation could relate to, one that made them feel seen and heard. A brand that celebrated our strong culture and protected it.

Now, how did I build Ah-Shi Beauty? I started with research. I studied the industry, learning the good, the bad, and the ugly of what the industry holds. Once I understood the landscape, I came up with a business plan, drawing from my upbringing and the systems I grew up with. For example, we plant every year. Before spring comes, there is work you need to do to prepare. Like anyone who has prepared to plant, you have an idea of what plants you want. Planting crops, you learn patience and that you can control only what you can control. You cannot control the weather, but you can adapt to the weather. With the same mind-set, I sat down at my college apartment dining table in the fall of 2012 and mapped out Ah-Shi Beauty. You cannot control the supply chain; you cannot control the economy; all you can do is adapt. Our ancestors were experts at being creative and innovative. They showed us how to build something out of nothing with limited resources. I drew inspiration from their example.

Something else I thought a lot about when building Ah-Shi Beauty was what happens in the cook shack during any of our ceremonies. I used to watch and cook beside the ladies in my family, and as a team, we prepared meals for the ceremony and our community. Each of us knew our strengths and weaknesses, and we worked together to work as a unit. Our cook shack was filled with laughter and love, and I believe that is the reason why the meals we made tasted so good. I remembered these experiences when I was building my team, and they inform how we operate the brand—always with love and unity.

And that's my next piece of advice for you: though sometimes it might seem like there is little to learn in the day-to-day, there are valuable lessons waiting to be discovered—you just have to be willing to look. The tools I learned growing up on the reservation have made me the woman I am today. How we prepare for the new day before we go to school or work, how we take care of our livestock before the season changes, how we gather firewood in the summer and prepare for the winter months, how we plan our shopping lists because we do not live close to stores—I drew inspiration from it all. Even something as simple as having to collect water for the house and livestock taught me a valuable lesson: when you haul your own water, you know that each drop of water is valuable, so you learn not to waste resources.

When I face challenges in life or in business, I always think back to my Kinaalda (womanhood ceremony). The four-day ceremony taught me so many of the lessons I needed to live my fullest life. Most importantly, it showed me that I wasn't alone. I remember watching my dad prepare and protect my cake as we sat in the hogan all night. I remember hearing my parents, sisters, aunties, and cousins encourage me as I ran each day. Hearing their footsteps behind me and our voices echoing through the canyon walls, I pushed myself to run a little faster and farther. And now, as a thirty-two-year-old woman, even when I'm traveling around the world I keep in mind that I have my family, my husband, and the holy people with me always. I am a part of something bigger than myself.

I have a chance to continue to do the impossible. I share this story to encourage you to tap into a moment in your life when you felt supported, encouraged, and invincible. Treasure that memory. Carry it with you always.

What else do I want to share with you? Regardless of how hard things get, always remember there was a reason the Creator blessed you with this vision. Now it is up to you to build a plan to turn your vision into reality. We can help rewrite and reshape history. We all have the same ability to do the impossible. We are our ancestors' prayers that have been answered. Do not forget our traditional ways as we walk on Mother Earth. Be proud to speak your language. Continue learning our language. Wear your traditional outfit and jewelry. Take up space and lift your voice. I am proud of you, and I cannot wait to learn about your work, warrior.

May you continue to walk in beauty,
Ahsaki LaFrance-Chachere

MOCCASINS

By Taietsarón:sere "Tai" Leclaire
(Kanien'kehá:ka, Mi'kmaq)

As soon as you think it won't happen again, it does, mindlessly hitting you like a self-driving electric car in a busy intersection.

You're asked to be the brand ambassador of everything Indigenous.

Such is the case in my newest role as art director for a fashion brand. That's the thing with being the lone Native at a corporate gig—you're always expected to represent the entire community. This isn't the first time that I'm one of the few diverse employees in a sea of Sarahs from Connecticut. Hell, I've been asked to be on the cover of more hiring brochures than Meryl Streep has Oscar nominations. I can tell things will be no different in my newest endeavor.

But I don't care. I made it. After all the years of interning, taking on odd freelance jobs, and Instagram networking, I'm *finally* an art director. I climbed the corporate ladder, from intern to graphic designer, and now I'm an art director! The degree paid off! (Not paid paid, of course—there's still decades of debt ahead of me.)

It's one of my first meetings in the new role. I'm wearing my best Montauk-surfer-hipster-meets-Eighties "over it" prep look. I'm rocking a brand-new pair of checkered Vans that were just opened that morning. Soft green. They're gorgeous. I've prepped visual concepts for an upcoming seasonal print campaign and carry them under my arm like a piece of weighted armor. I glide into the meeting like Anne Hathaway in *The Devil Wears Prada* post-makeover: *Is that? A new Moleskine notebook? Gridded?* I imagine being asked. *It is*, I say, relishing my reply. I take my seat at the aging oversized conference table ready to begin.

They run the items of the meeting. Okay, this is kind of boring. No different from the meetings that were had when I was a temp a mere twelve hours ago. I reflect on how junior I was then. *He really thought he had the world in his hands*, I think about the naïve version of myself from yesterday. If only temp me knew how similar these meetings would be. What a dumbass. I open Flappy Bird on my iPhone 5 under the table as the work tasks continue to be listed.

"Chinese New Year collateral needs to be concepted earlier," the person running the meeting says.

Done, I think. *And it's "Lunar" New Year.*

"We'd like to turn the preview collections into a printed book, instead of digital. Is that doable?"

Easy. I'm close to matching my high score on Flappy Bird.

"Next on the agenda: we're launching a pair of men's moccasins."

The room goes quiet until, "Tai, that's okay, right?" It's the big boss. Talking to me.

I look up from my new high score right as the tiny digital bird descends to its death. "What?"

Everyone is looking at me.

"We're making moccasins—is that okay?" she repeats.

I don't know what to say. Why am I being asked this? Oh yeah, you're the red man. I can tell from the way she's holding the printed meeting agenda that she's eager to move on. The truth is, my opinion in this moment doesn't matter at all. We both know that, at this point, the moccasins have already been designed. They've already been produced in some faraway factory. As we speak, thousands of them are probably crammed together on a cargo ship the size of my reservation in transport to the United States. I'm simply the rubber stamp at the end of a white person's guilty conscience.

"Is that okay?"

The question lingers. The truth is, I don't have an answer. Yes, moccasins are traditional footwear of my people, but what kind of moccasins are we talking about here? Plains style? Ornately beaded ones? My new checkered Vans are cutting into my ankles, making it hard to think.

Do I own the design of moccasins? Does anyone? What's the difference between honoring and stealing? This is too much to handle. Especially now that the Chopt salad I just ate is turning my stomach inside out. My delicate Native stomach. I wonder what my ancestors would think of me at that moment. Sitting in a conference room on the fourteenth floor of a skyscraper in Manhattan, a building that was probably built by the ironworkers from my own community forty years earlier, trying to answer my boss's question as I start to strategize the fastest walk to the good bathroom.

"Tai?"

I didn't answer fast enough. Now it's awkward. The silence is deafening. I manage to mutter something: "Can I see them?"

She pretends to be excited by my question and starts going through the folder in front of her. "Here they are," she says as she holds up a printout.

Yep. There it is. Basic moccasins that look like a pair I would have gotten made for me back home. The difference is, these have rubber soles for all those laborious trips from a Volvo to the front door of a Whole Foods. They're nice. I'd wear them. I also know that in exactly twelve months, they'll sit on a sale rack with a sign that reads: ADDITIONAL 15% OFF SALE ITEMS. The ones that aren't sold will probably be tossed or, if we're lucky, donated. Not to any reservation or Indigenous community that could use them, of course.

"Tai?"

I get up. "Would you mind coming back to this? I need to use the restroom." As I quickly exit, a trickle of blood from the back of my ankle begins to stain my brand-new shoe.

WE, THE
ORIGINAL STORYTELLERS

By Princess Daazhraii Johnson

(Neets'aii Gwich'in)

The lens was pointed at us

We had no say in what was captured

Constantly contorting to suit a foreign gaze

We became the romantic façade of American genocide

Stoic, unsmiling, a relic of the past

They presumed our extinction

Instead, we continued to sing

Even as we were torn from our homelands

Even as our children were stolen

We prayed in our language

We carried seeds and stories and medicine

And one day, we picked up the lens
To the horror of the Colonizer
We leaped from the old tintype
We, in fact, still persisted
Three-dimensional and in a rainbow of colors
Smiling deep and laughing hard

We found healing in telling our true histories
In determining how we wanted to be seen
In seeking justice
In protecting lands and waters and our own children

Projecting into existence the vision
We hold for an Indigenous Future
We, the original storytellers of these lands

It is 1980 in Anchorage, Alaska. I am eight years old and attending Mountain View Elementary School. My mother has sent me to school in two long braids. I'm an incredibly shy child. I have yet to find my voice. On the playground, a blond boy and his friend chase me. Instinctively, I run. Am I being included in a game of tag I didn't sign up for? While they laugh, it dawns on me that I am not a participant in a game of tag; instead, I am an object—their target. A terror pulses through me. The boy grabs my braids like the reins on a horse and makes a whooping-like cry, the supposed war cry we all recognize from the old Westerns that afflict screens around the world. The sense of shame and humiliation I feel has no language. It permeates my sense of well-being, my self-worth. If this is how I am visible to the world, I'd rather remain invisible. There is no one here to come to my aid, to right the wrong, to educate, to be a good ally or good human being. This interaction is an emanation of the consumption of racist and stereotypical images that are deeply engrained in the American psyche. From earliest paintings, written descriptions, policy, law, dime novels, songs, films, and television. The intentional dehumanization of the Indigenous Peoples is at the core of the issues we face, and the violence enacted on us and the land is intertwined.

It would take decades for me to learn the true history of what my family and ancestors had experienced through the colonization and assimilationist policies of the US government aimed at destroying our cultural identities. My first insight came from a conversation around Dinjii Zhuh K'yaa—our Gwich'in language. I was about thirteen years old, and I had grown up listening to my mother and aunties and other relatives all fluently speaking the language, though they never made any effort to teach us. At that time, I was also questioning life and my own identity and struggling to figure out where I fit in. Not understanding the language was making me feel left out of my own culture. So, I asked my mom, "Mom, why didn't you ever teach us?" She paused and then dropped this shocking response: "Well, I was sent to boarding school when I was five years old, and I was hit by the matrons when I spoke Gwich'in. So, I thought if you kids were going to be successful in a white man's world, then you had to speak English."

I still cry when I tell this story because I see clearly my beautiful mother at the age of five, anchored in her language and culture and being punished for being born Native—the trauma we have all endured. I cry not just for my mother and my generation, but for the thousands of Indigenous children stolen the world over and especially for the ones who never made it back home. The years of forced sterilization of our women, stolen lands, our bodies used as medical experiments, the contamination of waters and lands, our babies taken away at birth . . . These injustices linger as they continue to persist into our present-day experience. I would spend much of my teen years processing the anger and rage of experiencing and seeing firsthand the injustices imposed upon us, all aimed at tearing us away from our homelands to get to oil, timber, and minerals and simultaneously at dehumanizing us.

In less than a century, they managed to deplete and endanger our fisheries, waters, timber, and wildlife, all of which we had been in respectful relationships with for thousands of years. Through my late teens and early twenties, I found myself time and again using poetry, dance, theatre, and storytelling as a vital form of self-expression and healing. I realized that storytelling was an essential way in which my grandmother and mother communicated with me when I was growing up. My mother thrived in using our rich oral storytelling tradition as a tool to relay our values and spark my imagination. She also shared with me her love for stories from around the world. I had other powerful influences to help me to understand the underpinnings and roots of our own caste system in America, particularly the spoken word poetry scene of the Nineties in Washington, DC, which instilled a desire in me to learn more than I was learning in college. Ultimately, this search for justice led me down the path of becoming an artist, and I began pairing poetry with moving images. I didn't know how, but I knew at some point I would create media to help empower us as Indigenous Peoples.

With all the new learnings came the slow spiritual understandings that would make a pathway for healing possible, for reclaiming a sense of wellness, worth, belonging, and self-love. It continues to be an everyday practice. In this way, all of us are survivors. Only with looking back through world history and with learning about the foundation of current unjust and violent systems built upon faulty ideologies like the Doctrine of Discovery, Manifest Destiny, and the delusional thinking that humans are not inextricably connected to our Mother Earth and all its inhabitants do we collectively create a better path forward. It is also our birthright to feel joy, to bring back ceremony, and to create new ones as well. To celebrate our deep connection to one another, the land, and animals, to do what we can to be and remain true *human beings*.

I've been blessed to work with incredible creatives from a myriad of different backgrounds and to benefit from programs created through the Sundance Institute, PEN Emerging Voices, Reciprocity Project, and Netflix/Illuminative Producers Program. I bring my own experience as someone with mixed ancestry (belonging to both my Gwich'in culture and my Ashkenazi Jewish culture), of being raised in a one-parent household, and of living a very transient childhood in Alaska. However, my path has been very circuitous, continuously unfolding at its own pace and surprising me with dips, turns, and meanders.

One of the largest and most impactful ongoing creative projects I have the great honor of contributing to is the PBS Kids show *Molly of Denali*. With a group of thoughtful and talented Alaska Native advisors, we entered the exciting world of animation grounded in prayer and determined to share out our Alaska Native values and a view into history from our perspective. For all of us involved, the series has been a healing balm, a restorative vessel of stories that give us the space to showcase our humor, joy, and ingenuity. In the show, we model how humans can be in better relation to one another, our plant and animal relatives, and the waters and lands on which we depend. Non-Native parents have reached out to tell me that their children have started thanking the plants and learning our Native songs and dances, and Native parents tell me their child has become much more interested and prouder of their Native heritage since the show came out. One little girl saw the premiere and then ran home and started rummaging through her closet to pull out her qaspeq (like the red garment Molly wears on the show) and announced she wanted to wear it to school like Molly! These are the sort of value-laden ways of receiving story that all of us prayed for. To see our children recognizing themselves on-screen and to feel a sense of "Yes, that is me and my community and we are amazing!" is everything.

Building healthy communities rooted in shared understanding and Indigenous values is critical as we humans navigate this state of climate emergency. Not only is the act of storytelling paramount to elevating the issues we are facing, but the stories also help us lean into and express our grief, hope, concerns, and visions for what the future may look like. What might we learn if we only listened? In our traditional stories, we knew how to speak the same language as the plants and animals. We knew how to time travel and how to live with the utmost respect for one another. Through listening, we restore relationships. And if we find that stillness, that peace deep within, we might even be gifted with a story to tell. As I write this, the łuk choo (king salmon) are finding their way up the Yukon River, but their numbers are dwindling, and we are unable to set our nets. Our fate is linked to them and these lands and waters we depend upon. How might storytelling help our world realize that we are all connected and that we must transition off fossil fuels? There is still so much to celebrate in this beautiful world, and there is so much we can do to be better children to our Mother Earth.

I'll share a dream I had years ago. I was on a path that spiraled down into the earth. I was so curious and reached a point where the light cut off and there was nothing but darkness. I wanted to go farther, but I couldn't see. Suddenly, a large being—an ancestor—was before me. They were genderless, powerful, and beautiful. They were seated, but I could tell they would be maybe eight feet tall if standing. And they were humorous! They were laughing and teasing me about going farther down the path. So as not to be seen as being afraid, I stepped into the darkness. Immediately, I felt like I was being swept up in a large wave. I was spun and tossed around and around and then found myself spit out at the feet of the ancestor. It was so hard for me to stand up, and I asked them why. They smiled with kindness and compassion and replied, *This is what it feels like when Creator checks in on you.* When I'm feeling particularly alone or lonely, I remember this dream and remind myself that there are both seen and unseen forces who love us and want to see us reach our full potential. But also, falling down is a part of our journey! I aspire to bring this sort of loving encouragement to myself and others in the healing work we all engage in.

These thoughts I'm sharing here with you are at the heart of what moves me to act. To tell stories and to continue to seek knowledge. My work is linked always to the young Gwich'in girl who yearned to live in a world where she was seen and re-spected with love, kindness, compassion, and understanding. I hope these words are of encouragement to you. As we strive to be seen as fully human, for better representation, more sov-ereignty, freedom of expression, and protection of our lands and waters, we see that indeed our work is intersectional and guided by the strongest force in our universe: LOVE. Let us act from this place and let us breathe life into the most radical future we can imagine for our future generations.

Life will break you. Nobody can protect you from that, and living alone won't either, for solitude will also break you with its yearning. You have to love. You have to feel. It is the reason you are here on earth. You are here to risk your heart. You are here to be swallowed up.

—Louise Erdrich
(Turtle Mountain Band of Chippewa Indians)

MY FUTURE BEGAN IN THE PAST

By Sherri Mitchell Weh'na Ha'mu Kwasset
(Penobscot, Passamaquoddy)

I was born Panawáhpskewi (the people) and grew up on a small island nation that is flanked on its eastern side by a series of white-water rapids. Panawáhpskek (the place) is one of hundreds of islands located in the Penobscot River. Before I was born to this land, I was seeded in this ground. A dream nestled into the damp soil of this shoreline by generations of ancestors. Having been held here long before the missionaries, militias, and settlers came, I carry the untouched hope of those ancestors in my blood.

Our nation is one of the few Indigenous nations where we, the original inhabitants, have never been removed from our homelands. We have faced war, disease, bounties placed on our heads, and centuries of industrial disruption and pollution, and still we remain.* We have lived along these same shores for more than ten thousand years, and our connections here run deep.

Since the settlers and their armies were unable to remove us, they attempted to move the land around us, by re-creating the map with arbitrary lines. In 1842, the Webster-Ashburton Treaty drew a line right through our territory, forcing our northern relatives into another country.** This was just one of many dividing lines that would be drawn across the lives of our people. What follows is one tale of loss that helped me find my way.

Echoes of the Past

Have you ever listened to a song and been transported to another time? Heard a story from your childhood and suddenly found that the sounds, scents, and images are enlivened in your mind? Some words are held together with a magical thread that weaves a fabric of continuity between the genera-

---

*Spencer Phips, Esq, "A Proclamation," Massachusetts Historical Society, accessed January 16, 2024, https://www.masshist.org/database/6441.

**"Webster-Ashburton Treaty," Office of the Historian, United States Department of State, accessed January 18, 2024, https://history.state.gov/milestones/1830-1860/webster-treaty.

tions. When we sing our songs or tell our traditional stories and weave in aspects of our contemporary experience, we are transporting ancient wisdom into the ears of a whole new generation of listeners. This is how we ensure that our truths will stand the test of time. This is something that our ancestors understood. They knew that sound carries within it the vibrational frequency of life, and that the entire mystery of the universe could be held in one well-told story.

For millennia, Indigenous Peoples have utilized oral traditions to transfer vital information. Our cosmologies, traditional stories, scientific and ecological knowledge, cultural values, and histories have all been passed down one generation to the next through stories and songs. Cultures across the world have stories indicating that life was called forth with a song or a spoken word. This demonstrates the spiritual importance of sound within Creation. All faith traditions carry stories, songs, and chants that are designed to activate an altered state of being that transports one to higher states of awareness. The inner sounds of prayer and meditation and the outer sounds of chants and mantras are almost universally recognized as spiritually transformative. And so it has been for us within our own spiritual traditions.

For more millennia, our stories, songs, and prayers have been spoken here in our language, Latuwewakon. That language is both instructive and relational. It teaches us how to care for one another and how to be good relatives to all the other living beings sharing our ecosystem. Language helps a people understand themselves. Their understanding of the world is comprised of thousands of words that translate into generations of knowledge.

But what happens to the people when their words are taken away?

Growing up, I had the gift of language in my home. My grandmother was a fluent Passamaquoddy speaker. Her language is the language that first formed in my mouth, though she was stingy with her words. When she spoke to her mother or to some of the other old women in the community, she told long stories in the language, and they all laughed and laughed until they cried. When she spoke to us, it was only with the most rudimentary language. We learned a series of questions and responses that were tied to meeting our immediate needs. We understood commands issued by our grandparents, knew how to politely greet our relatives, and we could turn a few colorful phrases. But we were never given enough to be fully conversational. When I was a teenager, I started to pester my grandmother to teach me how to speak more of the language. Whenever I asked, she had an excuse for why she couldn't teach me: *I speak the language in the old way, not like you younger people do today. I don't know how to teach the language. I'm too busy for that kind of thing anyway.* Eventually, I got frustrated and stopped asking. For a long time, I took her refusal personally, and was hurt by it. Then, someone sat me down and told me her story.

My grandmother, Eleanor Mary (Dana) Mitchell, was born and raised on the Passamaquoddy reservation at Sipayik, which is located about two and a half hours east of the reservation where I grew up. She was the only child of Mildred (Dana) Ranco and was largely raised by her maternal great-grandmother, a woman named Nancy Dana. Nancy had never learned to speak English, so my grandmother was raised with the Passamaquoddy language.

When she was eight years old, a priest and nun from the local Catholic church showed up at Nancy's house. They told Nancy that they were aware that she had a child living in the home and gave her an ultimatum: she could send the child to the day school on the reservation or they would take her and send her away to a residential school and she'd never see her again. Knowing that this was no idle threat, my three-times-great-grandmother sent her great-granddaughter to the Indian mission school. The year was 1931.

Forty years before my grandmother was born, Secretary of the Interior Henry M. Teller sent a letter to the commissioner

of Indian affairs, Hiram Price.* In it, he described Indian dancing as "heathenish" and expressed dire concern over the role
of medicine men in Native communities. According to Teller,
the medicine men were keeping people under their control
and preventing parents from sending their kids to school. In
response, Price implemented a set of rules that became known
as the "Code of Indian Offenses" that were subsequently heard
in the newly formed Court of Indian Offenses. He outlawed
various ceremonial dances and forbade any traditional spiritual leader from influencing families against the schooling of
their children. The punishment for these offenses began with
the withholding of food from the community for ten days;
a second offense kept food out of the community for thirty
days and carried a jail sentence. These rules made it illegal for
Indians to be Indian.

In 1887, the new commissioner of Indian affairs, a man
named J. D. C. Atkins, expanded on the work of Hiram Price
by prohibiting teaching or speaking in Native languages in
all mission schools.** Mission schools on reservations were required to be English only. Any missionary who failed to com-

---

*Rules Governing the Court of Indian Offenses, 47th Congress, 2d Session,
March 30, 1883.
**"Timeline: 1887: Indian Affairs Commissioner Bans Native Languages in
Schools," National Library of Medicine, accessed January 16, 2024, https://www
.nlm.nih.gov/nativevoices/timeline/index.html.

ply with Atkins's mandate would no longer be allowed on the reservation. That order was later extended to all government-run schools on Indian reservations in the United States.

My grandmother entered the Indian day school a fluent speaker of her language. She did not speak or understand English. The punishment for speaking Passamaquoddy at the school was caning. Therefore, my grandmother spent the first three years of her "education" being beaten every time she opened her mouth and tried to communicate. Like so many other Native children, she was forced to learn English at the end of a caning rod. It was clear to her that she had not been brought to the school to learn how to read or write. She had been brought there to learn that it was dangerous to be skejinawok (Indigenous) in her own homeland. As a result, she remained silent for the next six years and left school in the eighth grade.

The laws banning Native languages and ceremonies remained on the books until the passage of the 1978 American Indian Religious Freedom Act (42 U.S.C. § 1996). By that time, my grandmother had grown and had daughters and granddaughters of her own. I will never know whether the passage of that law meant anything to my grandmother. What I do know is that even before this law was passed my grandmother was calling me *mishun* (her heart) and asking me, *Kil ona kotuhp, tus?* (Are you hungry, my girl?) and telling me, *Koselomol* (I love you). Though my grandmother continued using her language until the day she died, she never felt comfortable sharing it with us in a full breath, afraid that we would suffer like she had if we showed up at school with the language in our mouths.

Carrying the weight of my grandmother's story shifted my balance and altered my path. Before I was handed this story, I had been strongly influenced to focus on educational excellence by my grandfather. He was an administrator at the University of Maine and the founder of the Wabanaki Center, and he helped develop some of the first Native American Studies programs in the country. Though his impact on me continued to be strong, I also began looking around my community for more people like my grandmother, those who carried traditional Indigenous knowledge in tangible ways.

One of those people was a woman named Ssipsis. She was Penobscot and Mohawk, an artist, storyteller, and philosopher. In the decade preceding my birth, she organized protests about the injustices being imposed on our people, and she published a newsletter titled the *Maine Indian Newsletter*, a publication that she tapped out on a small typewriter in her home. She was fierce, and intelligent in ways that challenged colonial conventions. Some people were afraid of her, but I was friends with her three younger children and I knew that she was kind, creative, and interesting. She had real conversations with us about important things; she told us about the trees and the other plants and how the animals had helped us when we first arrived as a species. And she asked us kids questions that no one else bothered to ask, like when we thought the first snow might come and why. She had endless stories to share, and when there was a full moon, she would build a fire in her front yard and stay up all night singing and dancing. The old women from the church called her a witch. I was mesmerized by her. She was the only person in our community maintaining an open ceremonial life in my childhood; everyone else was still keeping their ceremonies hidden. Her son, Bill, later became our vice-Chief, and he was kind like his mother, always doing what he could to help the people.

Another traditional elder was an old man named Senabeh. He was a chain-smoking wood-carver who lived in a small trailer on the edge of the Rez. The men and young boys frequently gathered there to learn carving and listen to his stories. I wasn't allowed to go there. My grandmother told me that it was no place for a small girl, because some of the men there were drinking. Senabeh had passed away by the time I heard my grandmother's story. So, I didn't get a chance to spend any time with him. However, I had heard that he was funny and generous with his knowledge. I remember that he used to pay my cousin for his newspaper with a story, and my aunt would get mad and go over there and get his money. I think more than anything, I felt the absence of knowing him. He spent twenty-six years of his life living alone in the woods on one of the other islands. My uncle Wayne said that Senabeh had the true mind of an Indian. He could think much better in Indian ways than he could in white man's ways, and because of that, he could tell you things that only he knew, like the purpose of each living thing and how they could help you. Senabeh used to say that a person was just another element of nature, subject to the same natural laws, and that we had to remember our place. These are the things that we all wanted to know at that time. We wanted to know how our people lived when they were doing more than surviving, how it looked when we were operating closer to life. In his later years, Senabeh was arrested while holding a ceremony on an old Penobscot burial site, a location that had been taken over by a paper company. He won the case and became a bit of a local hero. He also had a lot of knowledge about the medicines, and people would go to him for help. Some called him a medicine man. Those things didn't go to his head; instead, they weighted him with responsibility. In his life he advocated for unity not only between his people but for all people. In an interview shortly before his death he said, "You can find unity in kindness, having confidence with other peoples, trusting people. That's the way."*

I didn't realize it at the time, but my grandmother's story was a rudder in my life, guiding me toward traditional cultural knowledge and those who kept it. It has taken me on a thirty-year journey with Indigenous spiritual elders and medicine people from across the Americas. It has guided me to my distant whānau in the South Pacific seas and led me into ceremony with relatives from the African continent, the Siberian tundra, and the Mongolian plains. What each of these connections has taught me is that we are all remarkably the same, despite our rich diversity and geographic distance, and that our core values and connective principles are alive and waiting for us.

Long ago, my ancestors planted the seed of me into Panawáhpskek soil. Our spiritual way of life, skejinawe bamousawakon, is held in our languages, ceremonies, and the many ways that we care for our relatives. I learned to walk this sacred path by following the shuffled footsteps of my elders over generations. When I place my feet in their well-worn prints,

---

*Pamela Wood, "Go Back Home, Senabeh," *Salt Magazine* 5, no 1. (August 1, 1979): 62-71.

I can feel my connection to them and to this land where they now rest, telling me that I too am Panawáhpskewi.

There have been times when I have longed for reunion with those ancestors, to be once again nestled into this sacred soil, cradled in the Earth mother's embrace, knowing that I would be rooted there with alder, birch, and ash, surrounded by the old families of our nation, Mitchell, Neptune, Francis, and Paul. Buried deep beneath the oak trees, down where I could hear generations of old women laughing and the steady thump of strong men pounding ash trees. Down where there was nothing more to do than to be still and listen—to the lyrical tenor of our spoken words and the steady hum of my grandmother's hands as she braids the sweetgrass for her baskets.

Psilde N'Dilnabamuk
I offer this for all my relations
Wolasuweltomuwakon, Uhkomi
I am so thankful for you, Grandmother
Kci Woliwon, kinsuhsok ciw Latuwewakon,
Thank you, ancestors, for the language you saved for us.
Komac Koselmol—I love you.
I offer this for my grandmother and all those who have had
their words taken.

AFRAID

By Trudie Jackson
(Diné)

My mind spins in circles,

Like it did when I was a child spinning on a merry-go-round,
my head tilted to the sky,

Escaping into my own world. . . .

Here, in the colonial world, I am often overlooked . . . passed
. . . glared at.

Oftentimes, I ask myself, "Is it because of who I am? Diné, a
person of color, a transwoman of color, Two Spirited. . . ."

Where do I belong?

I sometimes feel afraid to take chances in life.

I remind myself

To follow my dreams, to be who I am,

And remember my ancestors who have endured so much but who were resilient.

Stop being afraid . . . your time on Mother Earth is only a brief period so be who you are and make a statement.

And stop being afraid!!

TIMELESS WISDOM: GENIUS TIPS FOR ENHANCED NATIVE LIVING

By future Yurok elder Dash Turner

Honey, I'm so glad you're here. You literally look marvelous right now!

Okay, enough flattery. Boring! Let's move on. We're both here for a very important reason: you're reading a book about the Native experience, and I'm writing as someone who is taking the Native experience into unprecedented directions.

During my twenty-nine long years on earth, I've gleaned some sacred knowledge that is clinically proven to boost your life from "mediocre" to "unforgettable." And today's your lucky day, because guess what? I'm about to share some of this transcendent wisdom with you.

In three . . . two . . . one . . .

TIP: Try to be born Yurok.

I cannot emphasize enough how much better your life will be if your mom is a gorgeous four-foot-eight Yurok woman. We Yurok (Northern California's hottest and most popular tribe) are shorter and chattier than any other tribe in America. We are the divas of the redwoods, and we're #1 on any respectable tribal ranking for a reason.

TIP: If that's not possible, that's okay.

No worries if you've already been born and you're not Yurok. That's obviously a huge bummer but it happens. Whichever tribe(s) you were born into is probably okay or whatever. My advice is to find what's novel and interesting about your people and really make a meal of it. Let the world know!

*　　*　　*

(This extends beyond your tribe. Pay attention to all the different parts of your life, and identify what makes them special. Your hometown? Your dog? Your best friend? Your mortal enemy? You have to live in your world every day; might as well have fun with it.)

TIP: Do gas station taquitos the right way.

Now we're getting to the practical tips. Locate the dirtiest gas station you can find. It should look like it's been firebombed. Bonus points if there's a sofa poking out from the dumpster. Walk into the gas station with confidence and approach the plastic taquito box. Grab the tongs with gusto to establish dominance. You're here to win, baby. NEVER take a plump taquito—all that extra meat juice soaks through the corn. Instead go for the thinner taquitos, which are crispier and more satisfying. Eat the taquito within two minutes of exiting the gas station.

TIP: Try out a "waking up early" era.

No need to go full Jeff Bezos with a 3:30 am daily wake-up and ice bath. But I spent my senior year of high school waking up at 5:00 am for no reason and it was actually a blast. Everything's more serene, the birds are really popping off, and you automatically lower your stress levels when there's no longer a severe risk of oversleeping and missing English class. Live más, babe!

TIP: Take as many Jack in the Box napkins as possible.

Jack in the Box napkins are miraculous tools, God's final gift to the world. Nothing on earth is more versatile. Those things can sop up spills, put out chemical fires, and plug holes in sinking boats. If they'd had a stack of Jack in the Box napkins onboard, the *Hindenburg* wouldn't have exploded.

Grab thirty to forty napkins every time you're at the Box. If there's one thing I've learned from my mother, it's to try to live in balance with the world—and because Jack in the Box is a billion-dollar company, living in balance with Jack in the Box means taking as much as possible from them, constantly, without remorse.

TIP: Make "I love this!" your default reaction.

It's easy to fall into a rut of doing the same stuff over and over. Playing the same music on repeat, eating the same meals, et cetera. Yawn! Boring alert! Shake things up by always engaging with new stuff, and then bully the various lobes of your brain into *loving* that new stuff with one simple trick: say, "Okay, LOVE that!"

Say it after you ride your bike down a new street. Say it after you try cooking camel for the first time. Say it when you find a fully dried, years-old sneeze inside your library book. Say it when a woman starts chasing you around the Christmas-tree lot with no pants on. Give it a month and I swear you'll feel the difference!

By implementing this shift, you add 30 percent more happiness to your life and trick your brain into defaulting to this emotional reaction. Even if you don't manage to actually "love that," you'll at least be able to clock the humor in any scenario. Life can suck at times, but if you pump your brain full of "thought steroids"—like this mantra I'm suggesting—you'll make your mind way stronger and capable of deriving joy from anything. Another secret benefit? You also become way more fun to hang out with and everyone will adore you. Building a life around loving stuff (instead of existing neutrally or, worse yet, being a hater) is amazing. Can't recommend enough.

TIP: Remember, it's not just
Rez Natives versus City Natives.

As a College Town Native myself, the classic Rez/City divide is overly simplistic. Better to let go of dichotomous modes of thinking and embrace the infinite forms that Indians can take.

TIP: Learn to drive stick shift, if possible.

It's really cool and everyone will be impressed. Imagine you're in an emergency scenario and you're the only person in a group capable of driving that abandoned 1995 Toyota Tercel with a manual transmission back to civilization to get help. That's an alpha move. That's a Yurok move.

TIP: Get good at little stuff.

To build on the previous tip, it's really hot in general when people have unexpected skills. You might think I'm referring to high-octane/high-glamor skills like neurosurgery, but NO. I'm referring to little stuff. Get really good at crosswords, or piercing ears, or folding fitted sheets.

*　　　*　　　*

Getting good at little stuff is an amazing way to be hot to everyone around you—but it also makes life feel more doable. For example, I got really good at *Call of Duty* as an adult gay man (which is a #diversitywin and frankly an overcoming-the-odds story deserving of a major studio biopic) and it feels amazing. Plus, proving to myself that I could be good at stuff gave me confidence that I could tackle bigger challenges in my life, like filing my taxes or defeating Satan with kung fu.

TIP: Don't play football.

My mom "predicted" CTE (chronic traumatic encephalopathy) back in the 1980s and thus refused to let me play peewee football, and she was actually spot-on. If any six-year-olds are reading this: steer clear!

TIP: But watching football is fine.

I don't have a moral justification for how much this contradicts the prior tip. But waking up at 7:00 am PT every Saturday during college football season to the sound of my mother screaming, "YOU SHOULD FEEL ASHAMED!" at referees blowing calls on national television is one of my most treasured memories. If any girls or gays are reading this, please know there's legendary drama in college football and the violence is basically World War II level. It's like *Real Housewives* if the girls were given swords and encouraged to try to kill each other.

TIP: *Build up a spice tolerance.*

I grew up avoiding spicy foods. Picky eater vibes! The spiciest part of my diet was red Gatorade. Later on, I realized how lame it is to sweat while eating objectively unspicy foods like pepperoni pizza, so I conquered that weakness. Train your way up with little dollops of increasingly spicy hot sauces, and watch your mouth grow ever more durable. This tactic gave me acid reflux, but it was worth it because now I can go to Vietnamese restaurants and order the dishes with four red peppers next to their names. Rock on!

TIP: *Sunglasses give you the edge.*

Buy huge sunglasses and wear them everywhere. They'll block half your face so suddenly nobody can read your facial expressions. You're in total control now. *What's Dash thinking? Who knows!* This is how we get our land back.

TIP: Find your Tannhäuser Gate.

In the 1982 sci-fi film *Blade Runner*, Harrison Ford hunts down and decommissions escaped androids. As he's about to capture and kill a scary blond android named Roy, the android ruthlessly flexes on Harrison Ford by describing the badass things he witnessed in his life. Visceral images like "attack ships on fire off the shoulder of Orion" and "C-beams [glittering] in the dark near the Tannhäuser Gate." Marvelous!

IMO, we should all be a little more like Roy. Less so the part about being a synthetic android (although ripping phone books in half with cyborg arms would be sick), more so the part about embracing experiences you'll remember forever.

Nothing in my life measures up to whatever hot drama was going on off the shoulder of Orion. But I've had my moments, honey! I watched heat lightning for the first time from the back of a friend's Prius outside Yucca Valley. I played beer pong completely nude at a Danish hospice in Minneapolis. I snuck into a New Jersey sewage plant alone after a gay wedding. Your life can be filled with magic; stray far from the beaten path so it can materialize for you.

TIP: *Wear sunblock.*

As someone whose cousin coined the Yurok word for "man-boob tan," I am a bit of a sun exposure expert. I will simply say this: sunblock is amazing, and it feels way better to wear sunblock than to Google search "safe to pop sunburn bubbles?" and "sunburn bubbles good?" the next day.

TIP: *Add some throw pillows to the backseat.*

Time for another car tip! Tossing some decorative pillows (and perhaps a throw blanket) into the backseat is a perfect way to transform your car from a soulless commute machine into an eclectic living room for friends and family. Beautifying communal space? There's nothing more Native than that.

TIP: Embrace the middle finger.

Flipping off your friends and loved ones for no reason is so essential. Keep those losers on edge. Make them worry they did something wrong so now they have to be nice to you.

TIP: Don't let the universe win.

Look, bitch. What I'm trying to say here—what all of these tips secretly amount to—is that sometimes it can feel like life is happening to you. Don't let it.

I'm not sure if you're a big *The Price Is Right* queen, but most Indians are, so I'll assume you are too. That show has a game called Plinko, where the contestant drops a disc into a big, gridded board. The board has pegs that bounce the disc around. You have no control over where the disc goes. But as the disc falls, you pray that fate pushes it toward the exact center so you can win $10,000.

Life can feel like a game of Plinko, just a bunch of pegs pushing you around as you fall toward a random slot. But it's not.

Your life is a concatenation of your choices. How you start your day, how you treat the people around you, how you react to change. They all add up.

My endless and eternal homework for you is to try to become aware of these choices and make any adjustments you see fit. We're Indians, so we have the power to do that.

See, there's this idea called "linguistic relativity." It says the ways languages are built (and all their different words, concepts, and tendencies) shape their speakers' worldviews. Many Native folks don't speak our tribal languages—I can only say three words in Yurok and two of them are "manboob tan." But get this: our people's unique worldviews are still passed down through our families. Thousands of years of culture made them too sticky to be totally eradicated by some ugly priests who made our ancestors speak English.

So a settler's baseline emotional reaction to a problem might be anger, irritation, or impatience. But my mom always demonstrated to me how much more fulfilling it is to draw from a more Yurok emotional palette. Try to approach the problem with a little love. Laugh at yourself before someone else can. Ask your friends for help! If someone's being rude, feel free to hold a grudge, but be *classy* about it.

Your people's worldview can set you free, bitch! When you train yourself to have different reactions, habits, and behaviors, you force different feelings to the surface—and everything gets better. People are more lovable; music sounds better; sunsets look more orange (the best color). The world feels big again, instead of claustrophobically small. All those fears of loneliness, of losing control, of the grand universal Plinko board not guiding you to your desired outcome . . . those all fade away.

Because we Yurok know the truth: Plinko is trash. You're better off on one of the skill games.

TORY

By Mato Wayuhi
(Lakota)

At sixteen I chip my front left tooth on a bottle of rum

Tory speeds over a bump

on our way to a dance that

police would come to shut down

I lug a "fuck pigs"

jagging my smirk at their faces

Tory spares a fate

for the rest of my foul mouth

His pearly grace cools the cops mute

I owe him my all

he owes me a tooth to fix my broken house

Dad leaves to fight pipelines

Mom stays to corral her youngest

Tory drives us to his home

where our orchestra tunes

He touches me to sing my frets

I fret his strings to straighten

Tupperware nightfall braids boyhood across

granite countertops

Laughter warms a few

frozen teardrops loose

Lips chalk outlines of the fallen

Tory asks to hear my demos

We rush outside to witness

my becoming score his sunrise

His fingers jog a victory lap around my earlobe

whispering that one day I'll walk on carpets

redder than slurs he shelters me from

I say I will & so I have yet

I haven't yet found another

love great enough to misunderstand

Love that uglies

a slurring smile to safety

enamel tattoos forever enough to root speed

bumps across my mind

Even a wounded world is feeding us. Even a wounded world holds us, giving us moments of wonder and joy. I choose joy over despair. Not because I have my head in the sand, but because joy is what the earth gives me daily and I must return the gift.

—Robin Wall Kimmerer (Potawatomi)

MTV BOOKS SPECIAL THANKS/ ACKNOWLEDGMENTS

IllumiNative would like to acknowledge and thank our founder and CEO, Crystal Echo Hawk, as well as our entire team, who work tirelessly to change the narrative and the future.

Special thanks to Leah Salgado, Karly Toledo, Jessi McEver, Savannah Nix, Lashay Wesley, Robin Máxkii, Emi Aguilar, and Ben Kassoy for their care and dedication to uplifting Native voices.

We are also grateful to our partners at MTV Entertainment and Atria for their kind and expert support, with special thanks to Christian Trimmer, Rachel Thanasoulis, and Jade Hui.

RESOURCES

IllumiNative, https://illuminative.org

Career and Education

American Indian College Fund, https://collegefund.org

American Indian Science and Engineering Society, https://www.aises.org

National Indian Education Association, https://www.niea.org

Sundance Indigenous Program, https://www.sundance.org/programs/indigenous-program

Health and Safety

Call BlackLine—Crisis Call Line, (800) 604-5481, https://
www.callblackline.com

Indian Health Service, https://www.ihs.gov

Indigenous Women Rising, https://www.iwrising.org

National American Indian Housing Council, https://naihc.net

Native American Rights Fund, https://narf.org

StrongHearts Native Helpline, (844) 7NATIVE (762-8483)
or chat online, https://strongheartshelpline.org

2SLGBTQIA+

Paths (Re)Membered Project, 741-741 (text NATIVE),
https://www.pathsremembered.org

Trans Lifeline, (877) 565-8860, https://translifeline.org/hotline

The Trevor Project, (866) 488-7386 (call) or 678-678 (text),
https://www.thetrevorproject.org

QUOTATION SOURCES

1 *Our stories have the power to heal . . . :* Alicia Elliott (Tuscarora), *A Mind Spread Out on the Ground* (Melville House, 2020).

35 *We are enrolled members . . . :* Tommy Orange (Cheyenne, Arapaho), *There There* (Knopf, 2018).

75 *You never know what . . . :* Robbie Robertson (Cayuga, Mohawk), "You never know what could be interesting tomorrow," Instagram (robbierobertsonofficial), May 18, 2020.

119 *This is for every . . . :* Lily Gladstone (Siksikaitsitapi, Nimiipuu), accepting the Golden Globe for Best Actress in a Drama Feature Film, YouTube video posted

January 7, 2024, 2:35, https://www.youtube.com
/watch?v=BSapi-Og004.

155 *Life will break you. . . . :* Louise Erdrich (Turtle Mountain
Band of Chippewa Indians), *The Painted Drum* (Harper,
2005).

187 *Even a wounded world . . . :* Robin Wall Kimmerer (Potawatomi), *Braiding Sweetgrass: Indigenous Wisdom, Scientific Knowledge and the Teachings of Plants* (Milkweed
Editions, 2015).

AUTHOR PHOTO CREDITS

CONTRIBUTOR BIOGRAPHIES

IllumiNative is a national, unapologetically ambitious Native women-led racial and social justice organization dedicated to building power for Native peoples by amplifying contemporary Native voices, stories, and issues to advance justice, equity, and self-determination. By utilizing research, narrative and culture change strategies, movement building, and organizing, IllumiNative disrupts the invisibility of Native peoples, reeducates Americans, and mobilizes public support for key Native issues. IllumiNative works alongside Native and non-Native relatives and allies to increase representation across key sectors, galvanize support among national audiences, and build power for Native peoples to author their own narrative and their own future. Find out more at IllumiNative.org.

Angeline Boulley (Sault Ste. Marie Tribe of Chippewa Indians) is a storyteller who writes about her Ojibwe community. Her debut novel, *Firekeeper's Daughter*, was an instant #1 *New York Times* bestseller and received both the Printz and Morris Awards from the American Library Association. A Reese's YA Book Club selection, it is being adapted for a Netflix series by the Obamas' Higher Ground Productions. Her follow-up novel, *Warrior Girl Unearthed*, received five starred reviews and was a Book Club pick by Target and Barnes & Noble. Angeline lives in southwest Michigan, but her heart will always be on Sugar Island. Visit angelineboulley.com.

Philip J. Deloria (Dakota descent) is the Leverett Saltonstall Professor of History at Harvard University and the author of *Playing Indian, Indians in Unexpected Places*, and *Becoming Mary Sully: Toward an American Indian Abstract*. Deloria received the Ph.D. in American Studies from Yale University and has taught at the University of Colorado and the University of Michigan. He has been a long-serving trustee of the Smithsonian Institution's National Museum of the American Indian, president of the American Studies Association and the Organization of American Historians, and is an elected member of the American Philosophical Society and the American Academy of Arts and Sciences.

Eric Gansworth, S·ha-weñ na-sae? (Onondaga, Eel Clan) is a writer and visual artist from Tuscarora Nation. He has been widely published and exhibited. Lowery Writer-in-Residence at Canisius University, he has also been an NEH Distinguished Visiting Professor at Colgate University. His young adult memoir, *Apple (Skin to the Core)*, received a Printz Honor and was named one of *Time* magazine's 10 Best YA and Children's Books of 2020. His work also has been longlisted for the National Book Award and has received an American Indian Library Association Youth Literature Award, PEN Oakland Award, and American Book Award. Visit ericgansworth.com.

Kimberly Guerrero (Colville, Salish) enjoys a career in film, television, and theatre. Her screen credits include *The English*,

Reservation Dogs, *Rutherford Falls*, and *Spirit Rangers*, along with an iconic turn as Jerry's Native girlfriend on *Seinfeld*. Kimberly had the honor of playing legendary Cherokee chief Wilma Mankiller twice, in *The Cherokee Word for Water* and in *The Glorias*, and she originated the role of Johnna in the Tony Award–winning play *August: Osage County*. Kimberly has worked extensively to empower youth and promote wellness in tribal communities. She is the artistic director at UC Riverside, where she serves as an associate professor equipping a new generation of storytellers.

Somáh Toya Haaland (Laguna Pueblo) is a queer, genderfluid, neurodivergent artist. They are from the Pueblos of Laguna and Jemez, as well as being of Norwegian descent. Somáh earned their bachelor's degree in theatre from the University of New Mexico, where they pursued their love of movement and storytelling that was instilled in them at a young age. Somáh is a poet, photographer, performer, and climate justice advocate. They are passionate about using art and language as a vehicle to build new worlds. They currently reside on the East Coast as a guest on occupied Munsee Lenape and Canarsie lands (Brooklyn, New York).

Madison Hammond (San Felipe Pueblo, Navajo, Black) is a professional soccer player who plays as a midfielder/defender for Angel City FC (ACFC). She has tallied over fifty career appearances in her four-year career, which started at the OL Reign before she was traded to ACFC. Madison grew up in Albuquerque, New Mexico, and lived there until the age of ten, when she moved to Alexandria, Virginia, with her mom, who was active duty in the US Public Health Service. She became the first Native American player in the National Women's Soccer League when she made her debut in September of 2020. Since then she has used her platform to further modern representation of Indigenous people in sport. In addition to her work advocating for Native Americans she is an ambassador for Athlete Ally, a member of the Black Women's Player Collective, and her team representative for the NWSL Players' Association.

Born and raised in Alaska, **Nasuġraq Rainey Hopson** is a tribally enrolled Iñupiaq author and illustrator. She holds a Bachelor of Arts degree in studio art from Humboldt State University and is a student of philosophy and marine biology.

She's had several careers, including documentarian and schoolteacher, where her focus is always on reclaiming Indigenous culture and creativity. She now lives along the edge of the Brooks Range where the tundra meets the mountains in the arctic Indigenous village of Anaktuvuk Pass, Alaska, with her family. Her latest book is *Eagle Drums* (Roaring Brook), a Newbery Honoree. Find her online at nasugraqhopson.com

———————

Trudie Jackson (Diné) is an enrolled member of the Navajo Nation, who is born of the Bitterwater and Folded Arms clans. Trudie is a Two Spirit Trans elder, community advocate, and grassroots organizer for Trans Women of Color (TWOC). She founded the Miss Indian Transgender Arizona Pageant and the Southwest American Indian Rainbow Gathering. Trudie is a local and national speaker who holds bachelor's degrees in American Indian Studies and Public Service & Public Policy and a master's degree in American Indian Studies from Arizona State University. She currently resides in Phoenix, Arizona, where she has lived for more than four decades.

———————

Princess Daazhraii Johnson (she/her) (Neets'aii Gwich'in) lives with her three sons, daughter, and partner on lower

Tanana Dene lands in Alaska. She is humbled to serve on the boards of Native Movement and NDN Collective and on the SAG-AFTRA Native Americans Committee since 2007. In 2015, she was appointed by President Obama to serve on the Board of Trustees for the Institute of American Indian Arts. She is a Sundance Film Alum, a Nia Tero Storytelling Fellow, and IllumiNative/Netflix Producers Program participant. She is also an Emmy-nominated screenwriter and the former creative producer for the Peabody Award–winning PBS Kids series *Molly of Denali*.

Lady Shug is a proud Indigenous drag artist, born for the Diné (Navajo) Nation, raised in the Four Corners area of New Mexico. Lady Shug has been entertaining audiences for over ten years, beginning her career in Las Vegas. She felt called to return home to the Navajo Reservation and now lives along the Arizona–New Mexico border. As a community activist, Lady Shug works with grassroots collectives to fight for equal rights for her 2SLGBTQ+ Indigenous relatives. She has hosted a pop-up powwow in Bentonville, Arkansas, with Live in America, was featured on HBO's *We're Here*, and, in 2023, toured with Landa Lakes on the all-Indigenous LaLa Land Back tour.

Ahsaki LaFrance-Chachere (Diné, African American) is the founder/CEO of LaChachere Management & Publishing Company, Four Arrows Western Wear, Four Arrows Logistics, Four Arrows Saddles, LaChach Coffee, and Ah-Shi Beauty, the first Native American–owned and operated luxury skin care and cosmetics brand in the United States. Ahsaki has received the Native Business Owner of the Year Award, the Naat'aanii Leadership Award by Diné Pride, and the 24th Navajo Nation Council Fall Session Recognition Award, among others. She is a pivotal part of the movement that is resetting and reshaping music, beauty standards, and fashion. Learn more at ahshibeauty.com.

Taietsarón:sere "Tai" Leclaire (Kanien'kehá:ka, Mi'kmaq) is a Native American actor, comedian, and writer. His short film, *Headdress*, which he wrote, directed, and starred in, premiered at the 2023 Sundance Film Festival. He was a story editor and actor on the NBC comedy series *Rutherford Falls*, created by Mike Schur, Ed Helms, and Sierra Teller Ornelas. In 2022, Tai was selected as a member of the Sundance Native Lab and was awarded inclusion on The Indigenous List in partnership with The Black List. He is a former house performer at Upright Citizens Brigade Theatre. He has also performed at festivals around the country. Learn more at taileclaire.com.

Cece Meadows is a Xicana and Indigenous woman, whose father is Yoeme from Sonora, Mexico, and whose mother is of Tiwa descent from El Paso, Texas. Cece was born and raised outside of Yuma, Arizona, and currently calls the traditional homelands of the Piro-Manso-Tiwa people (Las Cruces, New Mexico) her home. Cece is the founder and CEO of Prados Beauty, as well as an Army wife, mother of four, published poet, makeup artist, entrepreneur, and philanthropist. Outside of work and parenting, Cece spends her time speaking, mentoring, and advocating for small business owners.

Sherri Mitchell Weh'na Ha'mu Kwasset (Penobscot, Passamaquoddy) is an Indigenous attorney, activist, and author from the Penobscot Nation. She is a graduate of the University of Arizona's Rogers College of Law and an alumna of the American Indian Ambassadors Program and the Udall Native American Congressional Internship Program. Sherri is the author of the award-winning book

Sacred Instructions: Indigenous Wisdom for Living Spirit-Based Change and has contributed to more than a dozen anthologies, including the bestseller *All We Can Save: Truth, Courage, and Solutions for the Climate Crisis*. She speaks and teaches around the world on issues of Indigenous rights, Earth rights, and transformational socio-spiritual change. Learn more at sacredinstructions.life.

A Diné scholar born and raised within the Navajo Nation, **charlie amáyá scott** (they/her) is dedicated to inspiring joy and justice. Their scholarship and writings are imbued with a desire for a more just and liberating education that supports and cultivates the next generation of queer, trans, and Indigenous brilliance. charlie reflects, analyzes, and celebrates what it means to be Diné, queer, and trans in the twenty-first century on her personal blog, dineaesthetics.com, and on Instagram and TikTok at @dineaesthetics.

Kara Roselle Smith is an Afro-Indigenous writer and creator based on Lenape land in New York City. She uses her platform to normalize the process of unlearning and seeking justice for her tribe, the Chappaquiddick Wampanoag. Smith's mother,

Alma Gordon, was the Sonksq of the Tribe and provided a strong example of leadership early on. With her mother as a model and her passion for social justice, Smith has created resources that have reached the screens of millions. Offline, she's begun work on her first book and works to secure reparations and recognition for her ancestors.

———

Vera Starbard, T'set Kwei, is a Tlingit and Dena'ina playwright, magazine editor, and Emmy-nominated TV writer. She was Playwright-in-Residence at Perseverance Theatre through the Andrew W. Mellon National Playwright Residency Program and a longtime newspaper and magazine editor for various publications, including *First Alaskans Magazine*. She is a writer for the PBS Kids children's program *Molly of Denali*, which won a Peabody Award in 2020 and was nominated for two Children and Family Emmys in 2022. Vera has written for numerous other TV projects, including ABC's *Alaska Daily*, Disney Junior's *SuperKitties*, and various Netflix programs.

———

Dash Turner is a comedian and writer. He has been featured on Comedy Central and Vulture and has written for *Solar*

Opposites, *Rutherford Falls*, and *Krapopolis*. He is an enrolled member of the Yurok Tribe.

Crystal Wahpepah (Kickapoo) is the chef and owner of Wahpepah's Kitchen in Oakland, California. She is an enrolled member of the Kickapoo Nation of Oklahoma. She was born and raised in Oakland, on Ohlone land, surrounded by a multitribal, tight-knit, urban Native community. She has received the Indigenous Artist Activist Award and has been inducted into the *Native American Almanac*. She has traveled all over the country attending food summits and building networks with other Native American and Indigenous farmers, land stewards, and chefs. Crystal values deeply the reciprocal practices of mindfully choosing Indigenous food sources with which she creates her cuisine. Learn more at wahpepahskitchen.com.

Mato Wayuhi is an Oglala Lakota artist originally from South Dakota. He works in film/television as both a producer and a musical composer, as well as writing his own music. Most notably, Mato is the composer for the award-winning FX/Hulu series *Reservation Dogs* and the feature-length film *War Pony*, which won the Caméra d'Or prize at the 2022 Cannes Film

Festival. He was also featured on the 2023 Forbes 30 Under 30 list for Hollywood & Entertainment. A recent graduate of the University of Southern California, Mato continues to work and play in Los Angeles, spending parts of his summers bumming around with family back home.